NORWAY'S NEW SAGA
OF THE SEA

Norway's New Saga of the Sea

THE STORY OF
HER MERCHANT MARINE
IN WORLD WAR II

BY

LISE LINDBAEK

and Others

TRANSLATED FROM THE NORWEGIAN

BY

Nora O. Solum

An Exposition–Banner Book

EXPOSITION PRESS   NEW YORK

EXPOSITION PRESS INC.

50 Jericho Turnpike   Jericho, New York 11753

FIRST EDITION

LIBRARY OF CONGRESS CATALOGUE CARD NUMBER: 69-17235

EP 46939

To

NORWEGIAN SEAMEN

Forty thousand sailing Norsemen,
One and all they chose the battle,
Homelessness and lonely ocean,
Chose to die from horrid gangrene
Or in flames on burning tankers,
Chose to drift on slender raft boards
Thousands of miles from help and care—
Deathless honor shall be theirs.

—NORDAHL GRIEG

Translator's Note

This translation derives from two sources: the author's book *Tusen Norske Skip* ("A Thousand Norwegian Ships"; 1943) and a manuscript somewhat different in size and content and partially roughed into Engish with the author's request that it be used. The translation represents neither the one nor the other wholly.

In intent and purpose and in essential content this English version duplicates the original. In other respects it admits drastic changes in organization, notably in its regrouping of articles as nearly as possible according to areas of conflict; in the elimination of material not wholly relevant to the main business or repetitive in nature; and in condensation. For help on difficult language problems it acknowledges indebtedness to Professor Theodore Jorgenson, a long-time teacher and reader of Norwegian literature and history; and on the English equivalents of military and nautical terms and expressions to Lieutenant Colonel Theodore M. Velde, United States Air Force. This help has been invaluable. Contributed articles have been given by-lines. All articles without by-lines are by Lise Lindbaek.

NORA O. SOLUM

1968

Foreword

Norwegians the world over are proud of the part being played by the Norwegian merchant marine in this war. They think that their seamen together with the armed forces are helping to tip the scales the right way and that their contribution exceeds what might be expected of a nation whose land is being occupied by the enemy.

When the history of this war is written, it will tell about Norwegian exploits everywhere on earth. The time for that history has not yet come and this book does not pretend to give an exhaustive account of what Norwegian sailors have done in the hard years since the war began. But I think it may give an idea.

Many more exploits ought to have been included. Some of them could not be related at the time of this writing. On the other hand, material of an unsensational nature has been admitted because it contributes toward a more complete impression of the Norwegian sailors' achievements. It is this view of the whole picture which is so important—the fact that all Norwegian ships beyond the reach of the Germans joined forces, that *none* failed.

To a large extent it is the sailor himself who talks. He does not use big words, but what he says is true. Every episode in this book is taken from real life. And the logbooks and journals which are quoted have the reliability which official documents may claim.

This role is of no small consequence in a time when Norwegian shipping and Norwegian seamanship are of decisive importance, not only to our own country but perhaps to the whole civilized world. I hope that this book, in the circles which it will reach, will help in opening eyes to this fact.

OIVIND LORENTZEN
Director of Shipping

New York
October, 1943

Preface

With World War II still raging in all its bitterness, and considering our ignorance in many matters connected with it, matters which for personal or military reason cannot at this time be made known to us, this book does not pretend to give any definitive history of the Norwegian merchant marine in the war. Such an attempt would be decidedly premature.

Nonetheless, one feels warranted in telling what Norway's merchant fleet is accomplishing above and beyond what statistics and articles on shipping tell us. Such records are as a rule read only by people with special interests and do not reach a broader public. A mass of material on ships and sailors, on individual and collective courage, has, however, already accumulated. From this mass I have chosen material in such a way as to produce a record embracing the widest possible range in subject matter and geography. The collection is a miscellany of stories from practically everywhere on the seven seas.

Insofar as its content has been gathered from many sources, the book is an anthology. All of these sources have been acknowledged. I myself have written about one half of the material. Through the circumstance of being stranded in North Africa for a long time while I was on my way to the United States I came in contact with Norwegian sailors interned there, and later I had ample opportunity to meet them in this hemisphere, chiefly when I was working as a reporter for the Norwegian-language paper *Nordisk Tidende* in Brooklyn, New York.

I have quoted from letters, diaries, logbooks, and newspaper articles. Most of the chapters are written in the form of interviews with sailors and have been checked by the persons in question. It would not have been difficult to find other stories equally interesting; the chief difficulty has been that of limiting.

Only a few figures have been given and very little has been said about the official aspect of things because these were judged to be outside the province of this book. The endeavor has been to bring to light something of the role being played by the sailors and the ships of the Norwegian merchant marine in the war.

LISE LINDBAEK

Contents

NORWAY'S NEW SAGA
OF THE SEA

NORWAY'S NEW SAGA
OF THE SEA

Setting the Stage

1

April 9, 1940 — And Afterwards

On April 9, 1940, the Germans made sneak attacks on Denmark and Norway. Without preliminary declaration of war they took over all of Denmark and in the course of a few hours seized every important seaport city in southern Norway. It was a violation of the most elementary statutes of international law, unprecedented in world history.

In common with the rest of the world the Norwegians were taken completely aback. The first few hours and days of the occupation saw them confused and irresolute. They required time to adapt themselves mentally to the new situation, to mobilize will power and organize action. More than a thousand Norwegian merchant ships on the seven seas received the terrible news on that day. Many cargoes were without ports of destination. Ships lost their owners. Crews lost country, home, and contact with families—everything which makes life worth living and sailing for.

In number of ships at the time Norway's merchant marine ranked fourth in the world, after the merchant fleets of Great Britain, the United States, and Japan. Regarded relatively, it was the largest: its gross tonnage per one thousand inhabitants in 1939 was 1,669, making it more than four times as large as that of second-ranking Great Britain; its population totaled no more than 2 per cent of that of the

United States. To this impressive fact may be added another: the Norwegian merchant marine was the most modern on the seas, more than one half of its ships having been constructed according to the newest ideas of the past decade. Its ships were very efficient and fast. In the tragic years of the early 1930's, when almost no ships were being built anywhere else in the world, the country's shipowners had shown remarkable foresight and enterprise in having hundreds of good, up-to-date ships constructed. About 60 per cent of Norway's merchant fleet was motor-powered, as compared with 22.8 per cent for Great Britain and 7.7 per cent for the United States. Norway had a tanker fleet of more than 270 vessels and a whaling fleet of more than 125 units which made annual expeditions to the Antarctic to catch whales and extract oil, and had floating factories among the largest in the world. She also had many refrigerated fruit carriers and special cargo ships.

Why did Norway have so many ships? The question is asked repeatedly, except by Norwegians, who consider the fact natural enough.

The explanation is simple if you look at things from the point of view of foreign-trade balances. Norway is poor in material resources. She lacks sufficient fertile soil for crops; her mineral deposits are few and relatively inaccessible. If, therefore, her people are to have and maintain a decent standard of living—which they want to do and are doing—they need to obtain a great many things from abroad. They must import more than half of their bread grain, four-fifths of their coal, and all of their oil and gasoline. Even if the country's exports were considerable, they could not earn enough to pay for more than about two-thirds of the imports. It is therefore necessary to earn money abroad to cover the deficit in the foreign-trade balance. Before the war there were hundreds of Norwegian ships plying as tramps between foreign ports, rarely if ever touching the mother country. One such tramp won the silver ribbon for record speed between Japan and China. An important part of the traffic between San Francisco and South America was carried in Norwegian ships. Several times Norwegian ships won the famous wool race from Australia to Europe.

This is from the point of view of national economy. But the fact that Norwegians prefer sailing to everything else springs of course from quite different causes. Only a very small fraction of the Norwegian boys who go to sea give any thought whatever to the balance of the Treasury!

Norway's coast line is so long that if it were stretched out straight it would reach from Scotland to Newfoundland and beyond. This it would do in its merest outline, without including the numerous fjords or the thousands of islands which lie close to the shores. In all of Norway north of Trondheim it has until recent times been almost impossible to get anywhere without sailing. The highway from the south to the extreme north was not finished until the summer of 1940 and it is still impassable in long stretches during the winter. Except for a few kilometers of railway from Narvik to the Swedish frontier, and two or three feeder lines at mining towns, the region north of Namsos, a distance of more than five hundred miles, is without rail communication. One can get to places only by boat; mail arrives by boat; doctor and judge must go by boat to dispense their services. Three-quarters of the country's population live within fifteen miles of the ocean. More than sixty thousand fishermen live off the sea directly and look to it alone for their livelihood. Thirty thousand sailors go to sea.

Probably more important than all this is the fact that Norwegians like to sail. They think it is no end of fun to be in a boat. If a Norwegian wants a pleasant Sunday or a good holiday, he unhesitatingly chooses to ski, swim, or sail. From early childhood to old age this is true—not because of his country's trade balance or coast line or shipping but just because it is plain fun. Every Norwegian boy along the coast—and often even the girl—has the feel of a boat under his feet. "The youngsters of the town were playing and shouting jubilantly just as they do in all our coastal towns where the play of boys in port makes them sailors before they go out on their first trip," says the novelist Jonas Lie, a contemporary of Ibsen and Björnson.

And so it would seem that Norwegians are such good sailors because they combine vocation with avocation: they sail because they love it.

On April 9, 1940, Norway had about 1,230 oceangoing ships, not counting the thousands of fishing vessels and small boats in her coastal traffic. On that day about 15 per cent of the former were in Norway or in some foreign port then occupied by the Germans. More than one thousand ships were in waters outside the sphere of German influence. As usual their men turned on the radio to get the news. Having by now become accustomed to the "phony war," they were of course expecting the usual message: "All quiet on the Western front." Instead of it came the incredible news: *"The Germans have gone into Denmark! The Germans have gone into Norway!"* A thousand Norwegian ships heard it.

The whaling fleet was homeward bound, loaded with a rich cargo of oil. One craft was loading her bunkers at Kobe. Near Finisterre a Spanish pilot brought a Portuguese newspaper on board a Norwegian ship and pointed to a headline stating that Norway had been seized by the Germans! A Norwegian ship in a convoy was nearing Norway, homeward bound for the first time in three years. Several of her crew stood at the rail staring toward the gray land emerging behind the fog. All were bringing gifts for wives or sweethearts, for friends and relatives. They were home again, at last! Suddenly an order flashed from the commodore ship: the convoy must turn back! Why? No one knew. In England they learned what had happened. The gifts for home did not reach their destination.

On a thousand Norwegian ships, over a thousand radios, and through thousands of newspapers, Norwegian sailors learned what had happened. The news was appalling!

an order flashed from the commodore ship: the convoy must
turn back! Why? No one knew. In England they learned what
had happened. The gifts for home did not reach their destination.

On a thousand Norwegian ships, over a thousand radios,
and through thousands of newspapers, Norwegian sailors
learned what had happened. The news was appalling!

2

The Merchant Marine Requisitioned by the Government

The more than one thousand ships mentioned as being
outside of Norway were owned and operated by about five
hundred shipowners or shipowning societies, with offices lo-
cated almost exclusively in Norwegian coastal towns. Altogether these had a trained staff of more than six thousand
persons. The effect of April 9 was to put their entire adminis-
trative apparatus out of commission instantly.

The complete loyalty of the merchant marine was never
questioned. Many sailors asked themselves in what way they
could best prove their solidarity with the homeland and their
hatred of the invaders. The little story of a Norwegian
freighter on her way from Pernambuco to Santos may illus-
trate. The very first act of her crew upon hearing the news
on April 9 was to repaint the ship, blotting out the Norwegian
flag on the side which had been the protecting sign of neutrality. The ship reached port. The crew had but one desire:
to go home and fight.

In Santos the crew aired their feelings. They headed for
Bar ABC, where German sailors usually congregated. A violent brawl broke out. The Germans were given such a terrible
beating that the Brazilian police had to intervene. Reports
came that a Swedish ship was leaving for Sweden the next

morning. All wanted to join her—they did not want to go to New York with a load of coffee. In the middle of the night the captain had to summon the Norwegian consul. He arrived at three o'clock in the morning and explained to the men that it was of utmost importance that they keep the merchant marine going. Norwegian sailors could do their country no greater service than to carry on at sea.

How was the situation developing in Norway itself? When the first and worst confusion was over and the King and Government had miraculously escaped the bombing attacks on Osterdal and the paratroopers in Gudbrandsdal, headquarters for the Government were set up in a small hotel in Stuguflaaten, Romsdal, on April 29. It was here that Mr. Oivind Lorentzen, as Director of Shipping, came to put himself at the disposal of the Government. The shipping directorate was one of four that had been established under the Ministry of Supplies in consequence of the emergency created by the outbreak of the war. At Stuguflaaten a provisional decree requisitioning the entire merchant fleet was formulated. This requisition was confirmed by a royal mandate (an additional decree) on May 18.

On the night of April 23 by order of the Government, Mr. Lorentzen, together with Mr. Arne Sunde, prospective Minister of Shipping who had joined the Government in Gudbrandsdal, left Aandalsness aboard a British cruiser. Mr. Sunde had been very active in military operations in Gudbrandsdal and had taken several German prisoners at an especially critical moment. According to one of his colleagues, he was the only member of the Norwegian Government who had actually fired shots at the Germans. The two men arrived in England without passports, papers, or British money; but they brought with them what was most important, namely, a document authorizing Mr. Lorentzen to command the merchant marine.

Meantime in London a committee of Norwegians under the leadership of Norway's minister to England, Mr. Erik A. Colban, had done some excellent preparatory work, even though all contact with the mother country had been cut off. Mr. Hysing-Olsen, who had been in Amsterdam at the time of the invasion serving the interests of the Norwegian Shipowners Association, took over for the shipowners. He was one of the few Norwegian shipowners abroad at the time. The German-controlled Oslo radio had ordered Norwegian ships to proceed to a German port; the London committee at once broadcast a counterdirective over the BBC commanding the ships to proceed to an Allied or a safe neutral harbor and assuring them that Norwegian vessels acting according to its directive would be covered by the common sea and war insurances.

The committee had already rented offices at 144 Leadenhall Street in the City and had adopted the name Norwegian Shipping and Trade Mission and the telegraph and cable address Nortraship. British authorities did everything in their power to cooperate. Their installation of fifteen telephone lines for the offices during one week end is one small instance. The most serious difficulty was finding qualified office help; eventually, however, competent workers were recruited, some from among Norwegians already abroad, others from among those who began pouring in over the North Sea.

There were difficulties of many kinds. In addition to the whaling fleet, Nortraship had to take over the management of more than a thousand ships; no one knew within a couple of dozen exactly how many. Nor was it known where they were or where they were going. There were scarcely any documents to go by, neither charter parties nor bills of lading. Norwegian diplomatic and consular representatives all over the world immediately informed the ships of the Government's requisition of the merchant fleet and required every captain to wire the newly established Nortraship: "I hold my ship on behalf of the Royal Norwegian Government." Telegrams to that effect arrived from all the captains.

Requests poured in for sailing orders and for money. The consulates did not command sufficient funds and the usual agencies naturally hesitated to extend credit to the ships. In the beginning charterers were reluctant to pay charter to the newly established "shipping mission," fearing that they might receive claims from the shipowners themselves. The first task, therefore, was to procure the funds necessary for the continued operation of the fleet. Every day that the fleet lay idle would mean a loss in earning power of not less than $500,000, even on a prewar basis.

The Minister of Shipping, Mr. Arne Sunde, tells a story which is typical: "Immediately after my arrival in London, I went to see my old friend Olaf Hambro, Director of Hambro's Bank, and explained the situation to him. After a conversation of a few minutes and without having seen any document or received any written guarantee he extended a credit of £100,000 sterling. I told him that we would not need it for more than a fortnight. And as a matter of fact we had repaid it before the expiration of that time."

A payment agreement was concluded between the Norwegian Ministry of Shipping, the British Treasury, and the Bank of England; and an official declaration was issued to the effect that charterers could safely pay any money due the offices of the Norwegian Shipping and Trade Mission. Money now began pouring in from everywhere; within six weeks the Director of Shipping and Mr. Sunde could jointly sign a check for £4,000,000 sterling covering the premiums for the first term of war insurance.

Many other problems had to be dealt with. The Trade Division, for example, had to direct the disposal or storing of cargoes bound for Norway. Some of these cargoes could be sent directly to North Norway, where the home forces were still fighting valiantly, but others either would be valueless there or were perishable and would have to be disposed of immediately. And supplies had to be bought for North Norway.

A stupendous problem was the whaling fleet, whose huge Norway-bound cargo of oil now had to be sold elsewhere. The insurance problem was particularly precarious, involving vast amounts of money. With the German occupation of Norway the cancellation of insurances in Great Britain had followed automatically, but the resolute and unanimous stand taken by the Norwegian captains made it possible for the insurance companies to work out quick solutions. They insured millions of tons of Norwegian shipping without knowing where on earth the ships were. Lloyd's covered one half, and other companies the other half; the whole transaction was negotiated in an hour and ten minutes, the largest insurance contract in the world! It is to the great honor of Lloyd's and the other companies that the matter could be expedited so quickly; and it happened, moreover, at the urgent insistence of the British Ministry of Shipping.

Another problem concerned the several hundred thousand tons of shipping under construction abroad under the accounts of Norwegian shipowners. What was to be done about it? Central shipping problems were of course taken care of by the shipping director himself; he exercised almost dictatorial powers.

Meantime events in Norway took their tragic and inevitable course. On June 9 the forces fighting in North Norway had to give up; Germany's blitz against the Western Powers, the conquest of Holland and Belgium, the collapse of France, and the events at Dunkirk having focused the world's attention on other areas, delivery of arms to North Norway was impossible. On June 7, in accord with the parliamentary resolution of Elverum of April 9, King Haakon and the Government left Norwegian soil in order to "continue the fight from abroad if necessary."

From a primitive and modest start Nortraship has grown into the largest shipowning concern in the world. When we look at its impressive apparatus today, with hundreds of employees and with offices in all the most important ports of the world, it may be useful to recall the first difficult days and to remember the many obstacles which had to be surmounted before it could attain this preeminence. Many persons had to brave death on their way to England. The chief of one of its main divisions reached England in this manner: On April 9 he was surprised by the Germans in Copenhagen. He rowed across Oresund from Denmark to Sweden. He covered himself and his boat with white sheets, and when German searchlights played over the water he pulled in his oars and drifted along with the thousands of ice floes in the Sound. From Sweden he reached London by way of Russia, Rumania, Italy, and France. During this war free Norwegians had to resort to many routes to reach their destinations.

The Norwegian merchant marine is run by Nortraship; it constitutes the financial backbone of the Free Norwegian Government. By a unique exploit the gold of the Bank of Norway was saved from the invaders. That gold has not been touched; it will serve in the reconstruction of the country. The income of the merchant marine is paying for our Army and Navy, for the gallant Royal Norwegian Air Corps in Canada and in England, for the royal house, for the Government and all its employees.

In what way is Nortraship directing the merchant marine? And what is going to happen to the ships afterwards? Mr. Sunde says: "Nortraship is an arm of the Norwegian State, and for the duration the ships are sailing on behalf of the Norwegian Government. The individual ship is being operated for a single purpose: namely, to make it contribute as efficiently as possible to the war effort without any regard to the special interests of individual shipowners. Whenever possible we have tried to maintain existing Norwegian lines. After the war restitution of the remaining ships will be made to their owners. In accordance with the Norwegian Constitution, shipowners will receive compensation for lost ships and for the use of their ships, as well as for depreciation of material. This compensation will be determined by the legal authorities after the return of the Government to Norway."

Other institutions essential to the welfare of Norwegian sailors likewise managed to establish themselves outside of Norway and to carry on in spite of enormous difficulties. After a surprisingly short time the Association of Seamen and all officers' organizations were functioning abroad, with offices in London, New York, and elsewhere. The Mates Association and the Machinists Association continued to be active. But the start was not easy.

3

The Norwegian Seaman

HIS SPIRIT

BY OLAV PAUS GRUNT

The scene is a classroom of the Norwegian Navigation School in Brooklyn, New York. Beyond its tall, shadeless windows gray shapes of factory chimneys and skyscrapers rise up against a pallid sky. Overhead, high in the ceiling, white electric bulbs shed a watery light over thirty-seven young seamen who meet in this bleak, uninviting room in a foreign country in a common desire for more knowledge and greater insight into their profession so that they may eventually enhance their services to the vital work to be done on Norwegian ships. . . .

A concept like "the Norwegian spirit" is hard to define. No purely rationalistic analysis of it can be adequate; it can only be felt intuitively and suggested through metaphor. But even the most down-to-earth materialist and rationalist, if he is sincere, must admit that the term has reality. One may not feel it so distinctly in daily intercourse with the average Norwegian city dweller in times of normalcy and well-being, but the war at least has brought it out, made it manifest in its purest and noblest form. . . .

"National spirit" often goes with chauvinism, with the bragging and boasting of blind enthusiasm, and it cannot be said that Norway, any more than other countries, has been free from such caricature. But our seamen, on the whole, do not like bravado. Almost daily the seaman's life is at stake in these times of war. Danger is his natural element; therefore he doesn't like to talk, and still less to brag, about danger. On the other hand, his familiarity with death makes it unnecessary for him to indulge in a pretended stoicism or in any restraint of emotions when circumstances call for them. He is not ashamed of his emotions. It is indeed striking how often one notices in seamen a great capacity for deep feeling, a sensitive, tender gift of love and devotion to things he has learned to cherish.

During long and lonely night watches, while the waves wash the ship's sides as she proceeds across the vast expanse of sea under a starlit sky, thoughts and dreams can roam freely. The kind of life he leads makes it peculiarly easy for him to keep memories of childhood, of visits back home, of the village and of the homeland, fresh and warm. At the same time distance and solitude help to reshape these memories, to give them depth and serenity. Details of less importance disappear; what remains is the permanent, the ideally beautiful—it is reality transformed by the dream of happiness and perfection which all human creatures treasure in their innermost hearts. The seaman re-creates in his mind a homeland transformed by the poetry of his own imagination.*

HE CHOOSES TO CARRY ON

The incredible news continued to pour in over the radio: *The Germans are in Oslo. They are in Bergen. They are in Narvik.* A strange foreign voice began coming in over the

---
*An excerpt.

familiar Oslo radio station, ordering all Norwegian ships on the seven seas, a thousand of them, to go to German or neutral ports in the service of the Germans! No Norwegian ship of the thousand and more of them obeyed these orders from Berlin and Quisling.

When Japan entered the war, the Germans renewed the effort. Again their Oslo radio asked Norwegian ships, particularly those in the Pacific, to go to the nearest Axis-controlled ports. Every man aboard would be given free passage home, a cash payment of 5,000 Norwegian kroner (about $1,250), and three years' wages. The result was the same. After several months of vain effort the Oslo station began promising the 5,000 kroner plus three years' wages to every sailor who returned home, regardless of whether he brought the ship or not. At this writing the station has not been able to report that a single Norwegian sailor proved corruptible.

On April 9 there were Norwegian ships in Trondheim, in Bergen, in every home port. German men-of-war blockaded their way out; in a couple of days German prize crews boarded every vessel. And there were Norwegian ships in Hamburg, Kiel, and Danzig, manned by German prize crews. The log-book of a Norwegian ship at Copenhagen had this entry for April 9: "No work was done on board today because of the political situation." Immediately after came the words "German prize crew." The Norwegian crew had been taken off and then brought on board again. A forced voyage to Hamburg followed; from there the ship went to Gothenburg for repairs. The ship's journal continues in the same hand, but the signature is that of a German master. Then the journal stops for a period. Seven months later it resumes with the laconic notation: "Since October 18 last year no ship's journal has been kept on board this ship." The notation was made in Glasgow. The ship, unarmed, had at some time during these seven months broken through the German blockade of the Skagerrak, gone to Sweden and from there reached a British port in spite of German command, German mines, German submarines, and the German navy. *How* it happened is told elsewhere in this book; the journal does not mention it.

On April 9 there were also many Norwegian ships in Sweden. Their owners in Norway were forced by the Germans to recall them to the German-controlled homeland. The ships appealed to the Supreme Court of Sweden to prove their right to sail for the Norwegian Government, which had requisitioned the merchant marine by the decree of April 22, 1940.

On April 9 there were many Norwegian sailors in Norway. A number of them were compelled to sail for the Germans. The way to Germany runs along the Swedish coast. Hardly a day passed without this sort of communication from Sweden: "Norwegian sailors have escaped from German boats and have reached neutral territory." They escaped in lifeboats and on rafts or swam ashore. Some drowned. But they escaped from the Germans.

During the armistice between Germany and France in the summer of 1940 hundreds of Norwegian sailors were forced into inactivity in France and North Africa. When they began to understand what was happening, that they were to be immobilized for the duration, they lost no time: they escaped in spite of all prohibitions and threats.

Norwegian crews in French colonies were thrown into concentration camps; they were lured with promises that they would go home. Some were set to work in the sun and sand of the desert building the Trans-Saharanian strategic railway for the Germans. Many became ill; some died. When the Americans finally arrived, more than 75 per cent of the Norwegians had managed to escape by themselves. Of the others, without exception, everyone still in possession of his health had tried it but had been caught and brought back.

To date, almost three thousand men have gone down on

Norwegian ships in this war. They have perished on the way to Murmansk, Malta, Manila, and Guadalcanal. Their ships helped in the evacuations of Dunkirk and Crete. The first troops to arrive during the invasion of Madagascar came off a Norwegian ship, and the first ship to enter the port of Casablanca was Norwegian.

It is amply evident that other nations appreciate what Norwegian sailors are doing. Mr. Philip Noel Baker, M.P., Parliamentary Secretary to the Ministry of War Transport, declared in April, 1942: "Norwegian tankers are to the battle of the Atlantic what the Spitfires were in the Battle of Britain in 1940." Admiral Emory S. Land, Chairman of the United States Maritime Commission, speaking to a group of Norwegian sailors in September, 1941, said: "I think it was a British publication which said that the Norwegian Merchant Fleet was worth as much to the Allied cause as a million soldiers. Well, I want to say that this is no exaggeration: You are worth far more than a million men." And the British magazine *The Shipping World* on June 18, 1941, has this to say: "Norwegian tankers are bringing us nearly half our oil supply. The Norwegians had no thought of war when they built up this great volume of tanker tonnage. But their wisdom has proved our salvation. Had it not been for the tonnage of Norway and other Allied countries, we should have been gravely embarrassed in maintaining our supplies of everything necessary for the prosecution of the war."

HIS STORY WILL BE TOLD

In May and June, 1940, the Germans poured in over Holland and Belgium. Hypnotized and often quite paralyzed, people stared at the giant juggernaut moving mercilessly forward, crushing everything in its way. Individuals were as defenseless as leaves in an autumn storm.

I had been living in France for more than a year, partly as a correspondent for Norwegian newspapers but more actively as a relief worker for Spanish refugees and particularly for the more than one hundred thousand Spanish children who were scattered all over France in hundreds of concentration camps and who were in general very badly treated. I was working as a representative of the Swedish Women's Relief Committee for the Aid of Spanish Children and collaborated closely with other international relief committees, notably with the American Friends Service Committee. We succeeded in effecting some improvement in the terrible camps as well as in certain French departments—Brittany, for example, where I worked chiefly and where it had been possible to place many refugees in productive work in close cooperation with the local French authorities.

This work, as well as any other work of a humanitarian and democratic nature, was of course wiped out when the Nazi forces rolled in over Western Europe. It was awful to think that these poor Spanish children, who, either of their own or of their parents' choice, had been living in these camps for a year in preference to living in Franco's Spain, should now fall into the hands of fascists in this way. But in the circumstances there was of course nothing we could do about it. The flight of more than twelve million people through France, rambling along over endless roads without purpose or aim, trampling one another to death, is a nightmare too painful to think about.

Then one day over an anonymous station we received a message which conveyed very little to others who might be listening: "The fighting has ceased in North Norway; the King and the Government have gone to England." Though we were not altogether unprepared, the news came as a crushing blow —one more added to the many we had endured. The two months following the invasion had been crowded with awful and heart-sickening impressions, with doubt and fear as to the fate of our families and friends. And the consciousness that the fighting was still going on in North Norway had perhaps meant more to us than we had realized; it had been like a midnight sun over clouded thoughts. Was total obscurity about to come?

I tried to get to England but did not succeed in finding a way. No trains were running, no taxis were available. I started southward. My journey progressed with exceeding slowness on foot, in trucks, in ambulances, and I didn't reach Bordeaux in time. I had to turn back a few miles from Biarritz and Bayonne, the last French seaport on the Atlantic; the Germans had arrived a few hours earlier. I finally made my way down to the little harbor of Port-Vendres on the Mediterranean close to the Spanish frontier; I knew that liners for Algiers used to leave from there. Finally, after a wait of seventeen endless days, I crossed the radiantly blue Mediterranean. In spite of everything spirits on shipboard were high; we were on our way from helplessness and terror and brutality; we were leaving the slimy moral infection which the Vichy regime was already spreading over a crushed and utterly unhappy people. We had hopes of many things from the Black Continent; most of all we wanted to reach a place where we could get back into activity and *do something*—not just be doomed to passivity when the destiny of our country and of the world was being decided.

Most of the passengers were young Frenchmen on their way to join General de Gaulle. In first-class cabins far below deck there were fifteen so-called stowaways, persons who had been forbidden by the Nazis to leave France but who had been smuggled aboard by loyal Frenchmen and who were now receiving extra-good maintenance and care. In France the famous "collaboration" was already making headway, but it had not yet reached our ship! Even though France had broken down and given up, not a person among those on board had done so. The young men sang joyous battle songs; they were radiant with a courage and a hope which seemed out of date in that bitter month of July, 1940.

From old experience in Mediterranean ports I prophesied that the first thing we would see in Algiers was a Norwegian flag. And I wasn't wrong. There, as we sailed into the beautiful harbor past yellow rocks, dazzling white Arab houses, and faded green palms, under a radiant African sky we saw the most beautiful flag in the world, one born of sun and wind flapping like wings above a white ship. "A British flag," said the French, very sure of themselves, and my protests were of no avail.

When you are confronted with the necessity of holding a series of interviews for a book like this, you are led to many strange places. You seldom get into a home, because these seamen have their homes in Norway. For the most part you sit in restaurants and cafés, in a bar in Casablanca or a night club in Lisbon, in the cabin of a captain or the mess hall of the crew, at a bedside in a hospital or at a desk in a newspaper office. Reticence about their experiences is characteristic of these seamen; or rather, they do not talk about them at all. It is hardly possible for anyone not in the same situation to understand what these experiences have meant to frayed nerves—their unceasing strain on thoughts and emotions. Where you do find an exception, a story happier than any invented by Hollywood, it will be a simple, human story, unsentimental because it is genuine, and one which can hardly fail to appeal strongly to heart and imagination.

The story will often dwell on dramatic episodes, on the ships that go down, but it must not be forgotten that most of the ships arrived at their destinations. Some sailors who have sailed through danger zones for years will declare that they haven't seen anything, have hardly noticed the war. A few sailors are mentioned by name in this book; a few have received decorations. It matters little who happened to get into the limelight; all the others are of the same breed. We lost many ships. We hope they will be replaced. We lost many men. They can never be replaced. But hardly a Norwegian today doubts this fundamental fact: Norway had a thousand ships. She has about five hundred today. When the war is over, she will again have a thousand.

sailors are mentioned by name in this book; a few have received decorations. It matters little who happened to get into
the limelight; all the others are of the same breed. We lost
many ships. We hope they will be replaced. We lost many
men. They can never be replaced. But hardly a Norwegian
today doubts this fundamental fact: Norway had a thousand
ships. She has about five hundred today. When the war is
over, she will again have a thousand.

4

Norwegian Freighters Set Records

When World War II broke out, in September, 1939, two
Norwegian fruit ships of the 4,500-ton class lay in New York
harbor. Though not large as such ships go, they belonged to
one of the many special types of craft that have made Norwegian shipping what it has come to be. Both were owned
by the Mosvold Company—the one named the *Mosdale,* the
other the *Mosfruit.* After the first excitement of the declaration of war had subsided somewhat, both vessels were put on
the route to England. With refrigeration compartments they
were excellently equipped to carry foodstuffs and went out
loaded to capacity with cargo. They kept up a rivalry with
each other in speed, traveling by themselves because they
had to travel faster than the convoys. Time and time again
they set out on solitary voyages. In the beginning they did
not even carry a cannon for protection, and when the time
came that there were enough destroyers and corvettes to escort
the convoys they still went unprotected.

Their scores were just about even. That their speed was
good appears from the following letter, reprinted from *Reports From the Director of Shipping* of October 2, 1941:

CANADIAN PACIFIC STEAMSHIPS, LTD.

Office of the Chairman

Montreal, September 17, 1941

S.S. *Mosfruit,* Montreal

DEAR CAPTAIN:

We have noted that you recently completed a trans-Atlantic round voyage in 22½ days, and I should like to take this opportunity to compliment you, together with your staff and crew, on this very creditable performance.

May I also wish you continued success and good luck in your efforts to bring the war to a successful conclusion.

Yours truly,

E. ALKMAN

Secretary to the President

By that time the *Mosfruit* had gained a slight lead on the *Mosdale,* a lead which she kept for a while. But in June, 1942, a U-boat crossed her path and after a couple of torpedo hits, the *Mosfruit* had to give up her hope of ending the war with the blue ribbon for the most crossings of the Atlantic. It was a bad sinking, costing a number of lives. The sister ship, the *Mosdale,* however, continued to sail without convoy. It made no difference that her greatest competitor had been eliminated: she still didn't want the prize to go to anyone but the Mosvold Company, nor to any city but Farsund.

In July, 1943, the *Mosdale* had rounded out her first big jubilee, having completed fifty transatlantic crossings since Norway's entry into the war. King Haakon and a great many British and Norwegian shipping officials came on board at Cardiff and awarded medals to captain and crew. From the beginning of the war she had actually completed fifty-seven crossings. At this writing, September, 1943, the *Mosdale* is on her way to the States on her sixty-second voyage.

When His Majesty thanked the *Mosdale* for what she

had done, he emphasized that he would not make a speech, because seamen do not care for speeches. But he would at least say that during the war these men had maintained the good name and reputation for speed and safety which distinguished Norwegian shipping. Captain Gerner Sunde and others on board received the Medal of St. Olav with oak leaves.

Of other medals awarded, one went to the ship's radio telegrapher. The telegrapher in this instance was a woman; moreover, she was married to the captain. For a long time she was the only female telegrapher on a Norwegian ship. Now there is one more: one Kari of North Norway has also gone out as a telegrapher.

The romantic story of this Canadian woman was told by the New York magazine *This Week* at a time when she was twenty-three-year-old Fern Blodgett. It said in part: *How Fern Blodgett Got to Be "Radioman" on a U-Boat-Dodging Ship—*

. . . She came to Toronto from the little town of Peterborough in Canada's Ontario province. . . .

For a year and a half, three nights a week, she religiously attended classes at the radio school. Bending over the transmitter key, memorizing the dot-dash codes, she dreamed a dream that went way back to the days when a small, wonder-struck girl in pinafores had watched the Lake Ontario cargo boats passing and repassing: just suppose that a girl—somehow—could go to sea! . . .

Then one day the telephone rang and a voice said: "Can you pack and get to an Atlantic port tomorrow? There's a ship needs a radio operator. They'll take you."

When she trudged up the gangplank the skipper was standing waiting for her. He was a young Norwegian and not at all delighted about signing on a woman *Sparks,* but he politely showed her to her cabin and then remarked:

"You will eat at the captain's table—special privilege for you. . . ."

Today Fern has 16 crossings to her credit. On one of them an enemy submarine broke water just off the ship's starboard bow, and Fern thereupon became the first woman in history to wireless the position of a hostile U-boat. Another time night-flying Nazi bombers dropped flares nearer and nearer the ship as, unconvoyed, it slowly plowed toward a west-of-England port. But the vessel was so thoroughly blacked out that it received no follow-up bombs.

When the ship makes port on the other side Fern often goes ashore alone. "That," she says, "is more scary than being just-missed by bombers or subs. Those towns are as black as coal holes at night, and walking through their streets unescorted is no fun."

Like the Admiral in *Pinafore,* Fern also has trouble with her sisters and her cousins and her aunts. Not to mention her mother and father. . . . All the relatives say that Fern ought to have had enough of a fling at the sailor's life by now and be ready to return home and settle down. But Fern, sitting at her sending key, just smiles: "Not yet. Until Germany is licked, I belong right here."

The press had been invited on board a Norwegian tanker in New York harbor on a beautiful October day in 1943. After some conversation her captain, Reidar Henriksen, of Nötteröy, remarked: "The only thing we are interested in now is getting out again, for we wouldn't like to see anyone get ahead of us in the race." What sort of race was he talking about? But first it might be well to repeat what the New York *Times* had to say about the tanker:

They [the crew] were proud of this ship, that was evident; they were proud of their record of having delivered vital cargoes, and their pride was justified; the vessel was as clean as a hospital. The interior of the ship was handsomely paneled and would have done credit to a passenger liner.

Her engine room which appeared clean to inexpert eyes was pronounced "very dirty, at the moment, because we are overhauling some of the cylinders," said the chief engineer, Barthold Seines.

The ship had been built in Germany by German workmen using German materials and been completed in June, 1939. She had crossed the Atlantic forty-five times during the war, with and without convoy, and had transported 300,000 tons of high-octane gasoline across the seas. No other single tanker had carried so much gasoline to England.

In these times people got as many miles as possible out of a gallon of gasoline, and felt lucky if their motorcars got as many as fifteen. A four-engine bomber used a great deal more. On a bombing mission from England to Berlin a heavy bomber needed on the average a thousand gallons. This was a great deal more than a car used in a whole year; in fact, it almost equaled the amount given on ten A-cards for a year.

Ordinarily a thousand planes were just about right for a raid on Berlin. This required enormous quantities of gasoline, which had to be brought to England across danger-infested waters. Since the beginning of the war this one Norwegian tanker had, therefore, brought enough gasoline across the Atlantic for a hundred such thousand-plane raids. Her total for the four years of the war was more than 105,000,000 gallons of high-octane gasoline.

"The world champion among tankers in World War II" had once struck a mine in the English Channel and the port side of her bow had been blown off. Some of her tanks had been destroyed, but most of the cargo had reached the port of destination safely. At another time the ship had rescued part of an American crew in the Atlantic. After twenty-two days on a raft the crew were too weak to move when they were found. This was in a high sea, and two men from the Norwegian crew had to jump overboard to rescue them.

Otherwise nothing of importance had happened, said the captain. They had performed their duty and would continue to do so. The crew was proud that the port authorities in New York considered the tanker one of the best-kept ships which came into the harbor. "Upkeep is important, for we do not intend to let anyone get ahead of us in the race for the tanker fleet's blue ribbon," said the men.

They knew that competition for the ribbon was keen. Another tanker of the same line had nearly as good a record; and several other Norwegian tankers had then passed the 250,000-ton mark. But many of them are now out of the race, because 40 per cent of the Norwegian tanker fleet, a total tonnage of 800,000 gross tons, has been sunk during the war.

5

The Odyssey of Two Brothers

Two typical Norwegian seamen tell this story in a quiet, matter-of-fact way. They are brothers, blond, tall, and strong; they have a kind smile. Before the war they were third officers on ships of the Wilhelmsen Line. Their name is Björneby. Finn is thirty-one. Svend, twenty-seven, begins the story.

"My ship, the M.S. *Tirana,* was in a northern Japanese port on April 9, 1940. The day's news was so overwhelming and bewildering that we did not know where to turn. Our one thought was to get back to Norway to fight, but we didn't know how to manage it. Moreover, now that Norway was at war with Germany, the Japanese authorities did not know what to do with us either. First they spoke of interning us; finally they gave us permission to go to Kobe, where there is a Norwegian consulate. Deciding, however, that it would be better to give all of Japan a wide berth, we went directly to Australia. There over radio we heard the Norwegian Government request all sailors to stay by their ships, saying that we would be most useful to our country in that way.

"We left Australia on May 31 with a cargo of motorcars consigned to an East African port. On June 10, northeast of Madagascar, we observed a trader traveling our way. She bore the name *Aberkerk* and had the Dutch flag displayed on her side. She traveled much faster than we did; our ship was making twelve knots, the 'Dutchman' about twenty-two. When she came within about six thousand yards of us, she swung broadside and without warning began shooting.

"On their first salvo they scored direct hits. The whole ship shook. It was just at dinnertime and most of the crew were below eating. I was on the bridge with the captain without any protection whatever. We were totally unprepared, had never even heard of the existence of raiders and hadn't the slightest suspicion. No sandbags—nothing. But we kept going full speed. The men tried to get out on deck. The shooting was so unceasing that they were struck as soon as they came out. Six were killed on the spot and ten wounded. We continued traveling but could not get at our guns. After twenty-five minutes the motorcars on deck began burning; we had had to store them everywhere because we had so many. The burning cars threatened to set fire to the whole ship, so we had to stop moving. We had sent out SOS signals for more than a quarter of an hour, but the other ship immediately ran interference and as far as we know nobody picked up our appeal for help.

"Two motor launches from the 'Dutchman' came alongside. The men were dressed in German marine uniforms. We were not surprised, of course! They were heavily armed, had high boots filled with pistols and hand grenades. They also brought floating mines, which they immediately attached to the side of our ship so that they could blow it up at any moment. The first man to come aboard was a doctor. 'Is anybody wounded?' he asked rather unnecessarily, since the deck was littered with dead and wounded. We merely pointed to them.

"Within a few minutes the Germans took over. All of our crew except two were transferred to the raider. The chief engineer was left down in the engine room, and I remained on deck. The Germans had no difficulty in finding their way around since our ship happened to have been built in Germany and they were familiar with every detail of her. Very able people, I should say.

"Our whole ship was riddled with holes and splintered everywhere. Just above the waterline there was a hole big enough for a grown-up man to walk through. The engine, however, had not been touched—those Germans had had confoundedly good luck. In just half an hour both ships were headed southward full steam. The Germans were probably afraid that someone might have heard our radio appeal. Well, they need not have worried.

"After twenty-four hours we stopped; our dead were buried in the sea, and the raider went out on new adventures. Our ship, the *Tirana*, with a German prize crew on board, got orders to go to a certain position and remain there until August 1; if the raider had not returned by that time, we were to take the ship to the nearest country, sink her, and try to take care of ourselves.

"I took a good look at the raider and almost immediately it occurred to me that I had seen that ship before! Not only that, but our crew had actually played football with her crew a year before in Calcutta! I don't remember the whole name of the ship, but it ended with *-fels,* as many German ship names do. When I was allowed to go back to my cabin, I looked in my diary for all these details, but the page had been torn out when the German officers searched the ship! At any rate she was a Hansa Line trader of the usual 10,000-ton class. She had extra engines and turbines built in so that she could make much more speed than the average trader of that size—as our experience had very well proved.

"When we met the raider again, she was already carrying about three hundred prisoners from an English ship seized on May 13. Most of them were Indians from the crew of the prize. The raider herself carried a crew of about three hundred, all well trained. She had fuel in her bunkers and provisions for many months. We tried to worm a little out of them, asked them what they would do in case of serious damage to the engine, but they just smiled wryly and answered in a noncommittal way: 'After all, Japan is not so far away.' They were very cautious about what they said; they were not allowed to tell their names, nor from what part of Germany they came. All the same we got to know considerable during the many weeks we were with them.

"When they had set out—they did not tell from where— their ship looked like a Japanese ship called the *Taku Maru,* with flags and neutrality signs displayed accordingly. Then she had been repainted to look Dutch. Following the capture of our ship, she in turn became Norwegian, Russian, and even British of the P. and O. lines. She never kept the same colors and characteristics for more than a few days at a time. Whenever necessary, big covers at the side could be let down in no time to hide the flags being displayed.

"The raider was of course equipped with all kinds of ultramodern weapons. She had two big cannons, one of them an eight-inch, and several small machine cannon. Every man on board knew with mathematical preciseness what he was to do in an oncoming situation. European prisoners were put in cabins; the Indians had to stay in the hold. The hospital was first-class and the German surgeon unusually skillful; he performed a brain operation on one of our men who we thought was wounded beyond hope, and he came out completely all right.

"As commanded the *Tirana* proceeded southward for about a week to the position indicated and waited seven weeks for the raider. Meantime we made all the repairs we could. We had a supply of cement on board and plugged some of the holes with it; for others we used wood. During our seven weeks at this spot we did not see a single ship—we were far south of the usual route. Had a Britisher arrived, our German crew would probably have tried shooting at her for a while. Later on orders came to sink our ship. But there was no sign of life.

"Our orders had been to wait until August 1, but on July 28 the raider returned. She had captured two more British ships and now carried six hundred prisoners, some of them badly wounded. There were also some women and children, all English.

"The Germans now decided to transfer all the prisoners to the *Tirana* and to take the ship to Occupied France. They helped themselves liberally to our provisions and fuel. The transfer of the prisoners to the *Tirana* proceeded slowly because of rain, wind, and fog. The visibility was so poor we could scarcely see a mile away. Then suddenly out of the fog a ship appeared."

Here the older brother, Finn, took over: "Two days before the German attack on Norway, I was on the M.S. *Talleyrand*, which had left Norway for Lisbon. We continued according to schedule and waited for instructions in Lisbon. From there we proceeded through the Mediterranean and the Suez Canal to Australia. From there we were to go to South Africa for coal. We had been given a route far south of the usual one and had been warned against raiders.

"For a long time we saw no ship at all. Then on a stormy, rainy day we suddenly discovered two quite near us: one a Norwegian of our own Wilhelmsen Line, the other a gray one without flags. The second officer shouted, 'Every man to his station at the gun!' The rest of us were puzzled to know what it could mean. All of a sudden the crackling began. I ran up to the bridge and saw the gray ship signaling to us. Then a second barrage. We started full speed ahead. The grenades hailed around us. There was no time for an SOS. The second officer was determined to fire. We had one 4.7-inch cannon, but the crew could not reach it in time. Had we fired, we would have been sunk on the spot, but at the moment we didn't think of that.

"In a couple of minutes a direct hit blew off the whole forepart of our bridge. The captain ordered us to stop. Then the gray ship hoisted the German marine flag, and a launch carrying heavily armed Germans came over. Our captain ordered: 'Clear the lifeboats!' and we stood there and waited. We especially noticed their small revolvers, small enough to be concealed in the hand. The Germans came on board, took command, and immediately sent us below; we were not allowed to come up. They seemed frightfully nervous and kept armed watch all the time. They were scared as the devil— feared an ambush, no doubt.

"The first night after our seizure we were pretty downcast. We had lost our nice ship. And the maddening part of it was that if we had gone a kilometer farther north or south, they would never have seen us. Our captain came down to us in the officers' mess and we argued back and forth about it a long time. Then one of the Germans came along, a tall fellow from Hamburg. 'Don't mind, boys,' he said. 'War is war. What about having a party in the mess tonight—all of us?' We didn't even bother to answer.

"Later that evening the Germans kept coming over to us and tried to get us to talk. The moment one of us sat by himself, a German would be right there with a drink; they wanted to pump information out of us. We asked if they always wanted to 'celebrate' with their prisoners. 'Only with Norwegians,' they answered. 'We ought to be friends. We all belong to the Germanic race. We wouldn't of course drink with the damned English.' They had no luck with us.

"We had now learned that the other Norwegian ship was the *Tirana,* and I thought perhaps my brother Svend might be on board. I signaled immediately to inquire whether he was there and whether he was alive or wounded, or needed cigarettes. I was happy indeed when they signaled back that he was perfectly O.K. The next morning everyone from my ship, the *Talleyrand*, was transferred to the *Tirana*. As we came alongside I heard my brother Svend's voice cry out, 'Well, Finn, this of all places to meet!' We had not seen each other for over three years and had a good deal to talk about.

"The Germans decided to sink the *Talleyrand* because she was older and more badly damaged than the *Tirana*, which had been repaired; moreover, they didn't have fuel enough for three ships. We had iron, wheat, and wool on board, and they took some of our cargo. They also had a small hydroplane on board and decided it ought to have some practice. It took the air, circled our beautiful ship and dropped a whole lot of bombs but did not hit her. So they blew her up with mines. It was a bitter sight to stand there and watch the *Talleyrand* go down."

Svend picks up their story: "After this the raider went off on new raids, and we began our voyage to Europe. We don't know all the details of what happened to the raider, but we did learn that two months later she captured another Norwegian ship, a tanker, took her to Japan, where she was repaired, and sent her to sea again with a German crew. She probably functioned as a supply ship for the raider. The Norwegian crew was put ashore in Japan. The raider herself was sunk in the Indian Ocean in June, 1941. She had managed to go on with her piracy for almost a year after she began planting mines south of Cape Town.

"The *Tirana*, with Norwegian prisoners on board and manned by a German crew, went out into the Atlantic far to the south and west. A few times a ship was spotted in the distance, and then we always got out of sight as quickly as possible. As officers of the same rank we brothers were quartered in the same cabin. This was the first time since we grew

up that we had the chance of getting acquainted with each
other.

"On September 21, 1940, we anchored outside of Arca-
chon, south of Bordeaux. Our radio had been damaged by the
bombing so that only the receiver would function; the transmitter was hopelessly out of order. Some of the Germans
therefore went ashore for orders. In a short while we got word
to go north and enter the Gironde estuary. We were glad to
reach land, especially in order to get some change of food.
We had had nothing but spaghetti and dried potatoes for a
long time, though there was plenty of food on board, for our
cargo consisted in part of provisions. But they wanted to
bring that ashore as booty.

"Now for the first time the Germans openly displayed the
swastika on the ship's side; it would have been better if they
hadn't. An hour before her scheduled arrival, the ship was
hit by British torpedoes. Three enormous explosions followed,
and the ship listed immediately. We were below in the cabin,
in our pajamas and ready for bed. We rushed forward to
help the women and children. In our haste we forgot the
life belts, and Finn hurried back to fetch them. The British
women and children were already on deck. A Norwegian
stewardess came running in her nightclothes. 'Oh, what shall
I do?' she cried. 'Just jump overboard with your life belt.'

"The deck tilted to an angle of forty-five degrees and the
motorcars on deck rolled off into the water. All of the Indian
prisoners were down in hatch number three. They tried desperately to get up the narrow staircase, but most of them were
crushed to death. Good God, how they screamed! One of
them was pinned between a car and the ship's hatch; his blood
spurted, and I shall never forget his screams. An English
mother with two children was in a panic, although all three
of them had life belts on. It was impossible to get to her—
just like scaling a steep wall. I shouted to her to jump over-

board—that then nothing could happen to them. But poor thing, she didn't dare and was drawn down with the ship. All three drowned. About an hour later we found the body of the little boy. He was such a pretty little fellow.

"I looked for the wounded English but saw that my comrades were taking care of them. Then I actually *walked* down the side of the ship and there I met a cousin of ours who had come aboard in Australia. Meantime I knew nothing about my brother. I swam clear of the ship, which was going down with engines going full speed. Then I found two planks, and having no life belt, held them under my arms. None of the lifeboats could be lowered in time, since the *Tirana* went to the bottom in two and a half minutes, but some of the boats came to the surface again and we either got into them or clung to their sides. Some rafts which had been fastened to the ship also came up. One of them was full of Indians.

"We remained in the water and waited for help. A German Red Cross airplane came swiftly, dropped lifesaving vests, and took twenty of the most seriously wounded to land. Three hours later a German mine sweeper came out and picked us up. The human toll of this shipwreck was a bloody one: eighty-seven persons had been killed, seventy-one of them Indian, six Norwegian, nine English, and only one German.

"Well, we reached Royan, and the Germans promised to send us home to Norway immediately. Our first week in France was spent in a filthy garrison barracks. Then we were moved—the officers to a villa and the crew to some wooden barracks. The Germans guarded us closely and accompanied us to town whenever we wanted to buy something. We were given forty pfennigs a day as 'prisoner's money,' but there was scarcely anything to be bought. We had nothing on but our pajamas, not even shoes or socks, and had to walk around town like that. The French were very kind to us. There was never any tobacco for the Germans but always some for us;

they gave us everything they possibly could, even if it was personally dangerous and risky to do it.

"Some weeks later the Norwegians in Paris heard about us and sent two of their women down with a partial supply of clothes and a promise to help us get home. A few weeks after that we were actually allowed to start, and since they could hardly let us travel through Europe in pajamas, they gave us some French Marine uniforms of excellent material from the military depot.

"The British bombed Royan almost every night, and as far as we were able to find out the town was without shelters. Every morning the Germans declared that nothing had been hit, even when we saw thick black smoke from a burning oil refinery on the other side of the bay.

"The most interesting thing we heard about was the invasion of England. The Germans, it was said, made two attempts in the month of September, the second of them in the Bristol Channel. We talked with the boys who had taken part. They had used flat prams, like the ones we saw on the rivers of France and Germany. But the British had pumped oil on the sea and set fire to it, so that the Germans had had to withdraw with enormous losses. 'We lost the war that time,' they would often say to each other.

"We went home through Germany and Sweden. We were afraid we might be held in Germany, and don't you suppose they offered us work on a river boat on the Rhine, which we refused with contempt, reminding them that we were seamen and couldn't splash around inland.

"We arrived in Norway early in December of 1940. We were put off the train at Ljan—where the Germans had built a new railway station—thinking presumably that our French uniforms might attract too much attention in Oslo. My brother and I boarded a bus for home, and who should be on the bus but Mother! A fortnight ago my parents had received a letter from us from France, so they knew we were alive, but they had not of course expected to have us home for Christmas—and in French uniforms.

"In Norway there was very little food and nothing to do. We were afraid of being seized by the Germans and forced to work on German ships, as many sailors were. So after a few months with our family and friends we decided to strike out again in order to be sure of fighting on the right side. Our parents agreed, of course. 'We don't want to chase you away,' they said, 'but under the circumstances we can't very well keep you from going.' So one day in April, we took our skis and crossed the border into Sweden. We can't of course tell where, but we knew of a good way to avoid getting caught. Most of those who cross the border are put into a camp right away. We managed to reach Stockholm. There we knew a man who helped us get the visa necessary for going farther. A short time later, along with four other boys, we left Sweden for Helsinki and Moscow by plane. There we took the train for Odessa. We had time to do some sightseeing in most of the Russian towns along the railway, and that was very interesting. Things looked much better everywhere there than we had expected to find them.

"In Odessa we had to wait for a time, but then we got a boat across the Black Sea. Eventually there were forty of us Norwegians there. At Varna in Bulgaria we had the pleasure of seeing those old acquaintances—the German soldiers. Thence it was across the Mediterranean to Cairo, where we got into a British military camp. By now there were sixty Norwegians in the company on their way out to fight. Finally we got passage on the English liner the *Empress of Asia* and sailed around by way of the Cape of Good Hope to New York."

The two Björneby brothers later signed as second mates on ships of their old Wilhelmsen Line. They will continue to have adventures to talk about until the war is over.

Scandinavia and the British Isles

6

Through the Skagerrak Blockade

BY JÖRGEN JUVE

Late one afternoon during a dense snowfall a convoy of five ships drew past the pilot at Lysekil on the southwest coast of Sweden. Chance and strategy had in a variety of ways contrived to bring the five together in a Swedish port during the course of 1940. Since all were united in the battle for Norway's freedom, they had become as one. By secret means they had designated the leader for each ship; their crews were welded into a single unit under the strictest of security measures. To the best of this interviewer's knowledge it constitutes one of the finest examples of our joint action in the whole war.

The five ships, the *Tai Shan*, the *Taurus*, the *Jon Bakke*, the *Elizabeth Bakke*, and the *Ranja*, were bound for England, fully readied for quick action should it be necessary. The crossing through the Skagerrak was, however, without incident worth mentioning; the enemy was so little alert to what was going on that he was sacrcely aware of the strong little convoy until it was practically in port.

I don't know just what it is that brings Roald Amundsen to mind when I step into the cabin of Einar Fredrick Isaachsen, captain of the *Tai Shan*. It must be the clear-cut profile with its hooked nose, though the body is a couple of sizes smaller than that of the polar explorer. The glowing eyes have a familiar look, as of preoccupation with faraway new places and new problems. Round about on the walls of his cabin hang dear family pictures with one of the King and the Prince in the palace park right in the middle of them. There are also some pictures of the memorable occasion when he was awarded the war cross.

"Oh, yes, the road to it was a long one," he said. "On the sixth of March, 1940, I was on board the *Taurus* leaving Oslo for Gothenburg from which we were to proceed to Copenhagen, where the *Jon Bakke* was in port. At four P.M. on the eighth of April the *Taurus* left Copenhagen and three hours later she arrived in Malmö. On the following day, the ninth, the Germans seized the *Jon Bakke* in Copenhagen, took her to Stettin and put the crew in the concentration camp. One fine day later on the captain got orders to return the crew to the ship and get ready to leave—just to leave, no destination specified. The German officers came on board with the crew. Outside of Copenhagen they sent out a special signal summoning a motor sloop. After telling the captain to go where he pleased, the German officers boarded the sloop. That ended the German command, and the *Jon Bakke* went to Gothenburg.

"In Gothenburg, I myself transferred from the *Taurus* to the *Tai Shan,* which I had reached by train from Malmö. As captain of the *Tai Shan* I was invited to take part in conferences, which ended in our inclusion in the five-ship convoy.

"Though marking time in Sweden was in many ways very trying, it was also useful. It made for a sounder orientation on conditions in Norway and intensified the will of the men to get into the conflict. This became so general that when the New Year's greeting brought the message that we would soon be moving westward, the effect was immediately obvious in the liveliness with which everyone on board went at his daily tasks.

"One afternoon in a heavy snowfall and under pitch darkness we set out at about five o'clock. The logbook says we discharged the pilot after passing Lysekil at 5:45 P.M. on January 23. The boats were blacked out. Each followed the route which the captain regarded as safest.

"Later in the evening the first mate, a Swede, on watch from seven to midnight, came running into the charthouse, where I was, to say, 'Devil take me if we don't have a light to starboard, and I think it's a lighthouse.' Somewhat later a similar thing occurred. These proved to have been Lindesnes and Lista lighthouses [southernmost tip of Norway]. The mate concluded that either this was sabotage by the Norwegians or there were kindhearted Germans—which he couldn't believe.

"The next morning at dawn we saw the coast line of Stavanger, but fortunately heavy snow was falling over the mountains. At 12:30 as we were about to go down to lunch the captain's mate came to announce: 'There are warships straight ahead. What are the orders?' The answer: 'Head straight at them.'

"According to agreement, we raised identification signals when we came on deck. A large white flag with *G.B.* in blue went up instantly. The flag was British and the warships were British destroyers. Our joy was great. Now we had two destroyers, one fore and one aft, and one light cruiser on each side.

"As I stood on deck talking to the officers one of the cruisers began shooting. A hail of shots roiled the sea before our eyes until the fire from the cruiser shot a tremendous column high into the air.

"On Saturday at 5:20 A.M. the Kirkwall pilot came on board. I slept seven hours before we were in. Then one of the port authorities remarked that the captain needed sleep. He couldn't believe that I had slept."

Following are some entries from the captain's logbook:

"Anchored at 6:05 A.M. in the roadstead.

"Warmly welcomed. Trip 100 per cent successful. Except *Ranja* attacked by aircraft. First mate hit. Died later in a Kirkwall hospital.

"Left for Glasgow under escort. Had no charts. Navigated by overseas chart.

"Arrived at Gourock.

"End of voyage.

"Received by representatives of British Ministry of Supply and Nortraship.

"Steward prepared lunch for 22 persons in 20 minutes.

"Cargo: pig iron, steel pipes for planes, five cases of carburetors.

"Cargo increased airplane production in England by one third in one year. The carburetors sufficed R.A.F. for 18 months."

These slight entries tell their own story. The world now understands how it was possible for the R.A.F. to keep going. The Norwegian merchant marine proved a strong arm in the conflict—figuratively and literally.

The group reached a harbor in Scotland intact, unweakened, but not unnoticed. The British authorities and our own both understood what the exploit had meant. Awards in the form of war crosses and medals came quickly. No best-seller war book has recorded this exploit. The few scant entries in the logbook make up the only available document. Would that it had been more complete; it could, for example, have mentioned that under the very violent bomber attack on the *Ranja* all the men stood by their posts and repulsed it. These five ships have now continued in the service for some time, each plying waters in her own area the world over.

7

Traffic Along the British Coast

A Radio Interview

CONDUCTED BY FREDRIK HASLUND

Haslund. Today we are interviewing a young Norwegian cook, whom for the occasion we shall call Larsen. He is in the service of a Norwegian ship now in dock at an East Coast port of the United States. Since the outbreak of the war, however, he has been sailing along the English coast most of the time.

Larsen does not show any signs of having done a particularly dangerous job. As he sits here with us this fair-haired, blue-eyed young Norseman is calm and confident. His calm and confidence are due not to unawareness but to the certain knowledge that there is a job that has to be done. He knows full well what he is going back to.

How did you come to sail off the English coast, Larsen?

Larsen. Well, I happened to be on a ship which was sunk, and came ashore in England. I was in London a short time and then signed on a ship which was going over here. On the way we called at a port on the east coast of England. While we were there I spent a night in a second-floor hotel room. That night a bomb exploded in the square outside the hotel. The blast shattered all the windowpanes. Some of the splinters struck me here under the eye; and seven small ones were removed at the hospital, where they kept me for ten days. At that time there had, by the way, been three hundred German planes over the city, but the English pursuit planes forced them back and shot down a number of them. They did not do much damage.

Haslund. Did you go back to London when you came out of the hospital?

Larsen. No, my ship had left by that time and I signed on a small tramp steamer which sailed between London and Tyne. I made six trips on that. I think the ship had been doing coastal service in Norway but had escaped when we gave up North Norway.

Haslund. I suppose you were in constant danger of being bombed and torpedoed while you were in those waters?

Larsen. No, not at all. Submarines don't come in there and we didn't see much of the planes during the first five trips. They did, to be sure, bother us a bit when we were in port, but not outside. They flew high above us, but they never attacked.

Haslund. It was during this time that the great air raids on London were made, wasn't it?

Larsen. Yes, we experienced a little of everything when we were there. The ship put in to at least ten different docks in London at this time, loading and discharging cargo, so I had plenty of opportunity to see how it looked there. No really serious destruction anywhere then. Most of the bombs fell into the river in the residential district. Once ten or eleven fell into the river right beside us but did no damage. We looked on from the deck. During the raids we lay down on the deck to avoid bomb splinters. The watch was the only one who had a steel helmet, though all hands had gas masks. Often there were several hundred planes overhead. But the work went on. No cranes were destroyed, as far as I could see, and very few warehouses.

Haslund. Did you work during the raids too?

Larsen. No. While they lasted, we stopped, naturally. But you must remember that as long as they kept up the daylight raiding, they hardly ever managed to get in over the city. Later, when they began night bombing, it was different. Then they dropped bombs that clearly illuminated the entire area. Even so I remember seeing a real blaze down there only once. And that fire was completely extinguished by morning.

Haslund. Could you go ashore during all this?

Larsen. Yes, we had shore leave as usual—until twelve o'clock. It was while we were ashore that we had the most excitement. One evening on our way from the movies I had to throw myself down five times. One bomb fell fifty meters away from me, but it didn't explode. The movies were open, though most of them closed early; just a few were open until nine. Restaurants, on the other hand, and bars and such were generally open until ten. There was no shortage of whiskey either.

Haslund. But then, on the sixth trip things didn't go so well?

Larsen. That's right. We were in a convoy of fifty vessels, and just as we got out into the mouth of the Thames, we met another convoy of fifty, so that there were a hundred ships in all. Thirty big German bombers came flying right over us at great speed. They had been inland and had been forced back without having dropped their bombs. The Spitfires had somehow lost track of them, so now they saw a chance to make themselves useful. They flew low over the mast tops and dropped several hundred bombs, many of them small. They must have been in a hurry, for it looked as if they dropped the bombs anywhere just to get rid of them. But a lot of ships went down. An ammunition ship blew up, and I saw three

ships go. They said seven ships were lost, perhaps more. This
is supposed to have been the worst raid that was made. Then
the Spitfires reappeared and the German planes speeded off.
They vanished with a swarm of English pursuit planes at
their tails.

Haslund. And you continued on your way?

Larsen. Yes. I did not get back to London until a few
weeks before Christmas, and then I took a little vacation
again. I stayed there for three weeks.

Haslund. What was it like then?

Larsen. Oh, it was fine. We had a lot of fun, at any rate.
When we were short of money, we just went down into the
underground [subway]. There was always fun and entertain-
ment there. Actors entertained and there was much dancing.
And it didn't cost anything. They served coffee and soft drinks
and cakes, and we had to pay for that, but it was very rea-
sonable.

Haslund. But was underground traffic halted then?

Larsen. No, the trains ran all the time, but those who
wanted to board them had only a very narrow passageway,
because the rest of the platform was filled with people. Every
afternoon at dusk one could see streams of people with bedding going down to sleep.

Haslund. Did you stay in a shelter at night?

Larsen. No, two other boys and I had rented a room near
London Bridge. Together we paid thirty shillings a week
without meals, which we ate outside. We had ration cards.

Haslund. But I mean, did you sleep in your room at night?

Larsen. Oh, certainly. There were many who did not go
down but took chances. One evening we were invited to a
private home—six boys and girls. When we got into the hall,
a bomb fell right on the house. It was completely destroyed,
everything fell apart and rained all over us in the hall.

Haslund. You weren't injured?

Larsen. No, no one was injured, but we got frightfully dirty. The girls screamed, but they quieted down again very soon.

Haslund. What did you do then?

Larsen. Well, we went to a night club. It was a good deal like what it is at home after a fire, when one puts on the coffee-pot and sits down to talk about the event afterwards. Once, however, when a bomb fell right near the house where we were staying, we did consider going into a shelter, but nothing came of it. In the morning we discovered that a greenhouse which stood about fifty feet from our house had been blown to bits. Then we agreed that we would go into the shelter next time, but we never did. We did as we do at sea—took a chance and let come what may. But the landlady went to the shelter.

People often stood on the streets watching the whole thing. I seldom saw anyone chased in. I remember especially once in Newcastle when there was a big show. The British searchlights had caught a plane and held it until it was shot down like a flaming torch. Then the police tried to chase the crowd indoors, but it was useless. The enthusiasm of the crowds was such that it could only be compared to that of the final game of a home series.

Haslund. Larsen has not only sailed along the coast of England but has also crossed the Atlantic several times. One of these trips was so exciting that we must hear a little about it, too. Won't you tell us something about the event I refer to, Larsen?

Larsen. Well, it happened on the first trip I made with the ship. We were on our way back from Canada with a cargo of lumber bound for London and were approaching the English coast when a Nazi submarine came at us. It was midnight when the watch came down into the mess and told us to get our life jackets on. He had seen something. I went up on deck and at once saw the outline of a U-boat in the dark. She made a circle around us above water not more than about fifty or sixty feet away.

Suddenly we heard the command: "Ready—fire on board there!"—and then came the explosion. The first shell went right through the engine room. The oiler came rushing up immediately, but the engineer stayed below long enough to stop the engine and get the pump started. While he was down there, two more shells went straight through the engine room, though neither of them exploded.

Haslund. What did you do then?

Larsen. Well, I realized that this might be serious, so I went below and got my girl friend's photograph. They fired fifteen shells in all. One of them exploded at the entrance to the lumber cargo. Eight of us were standing there and the splinters rained around us, but none of us was injured. Then came an incendiary shell and before we knew it, all the lumber on deck was a sea of flame. Four of us sprang across the lumber and started to set out the boats. The first mate ran up towards the bridge; he probably wanted to send a wireless. But he didn't get there. Machine-gun bullets rained over him. He was shot in the head and chest and probably died instantly. We had no concrete reinforcement on the bridge then. We have now.

Haslund. But you succeeded in getting the lifeboats out?

Larsen. Not right away. We had to throw ourselves down into the winch hole, and there we lay for half an hour while the submarine fired machine-gun bullets. It was pretty rough going. We saw it plainly. At last it became so hot that we had to do something! so we took a chance—and made it. The first lifeboat sank immediately; it had been completely riddled by bullets. But the other one floated all right. There were twenty-seven men in it.

Haslund. Was there room for so many?

Larsen. Well, that is, most of us were in the water. The captain told us to hang onto the outside of the lifeboat, ready to duck if the submarine should begin shooting again. We were expecting that to happen any minute, as she was just a short distance away from us.

Haslund. But she didn't shoot any more then?

Larsen. No, in a short while she submerged. She didn't come over to us and didn't ask us about anything.

Haslund. Did you begin rowing or sailing?

Larsen. No, one man besides the captain's mate was missing, so we stayed where we were and called out to him. But we didn't hear anything and agreed to wait until dawn. About five o'clock in the morning we saw his head some distance away. He had been swimming in his life jacket all night and was pretty well worn out.

Haslund. And then you drew off?

Larsen. No, some of us managed to get on board amidships. We didn't have provisions and clothing enough; besides, we had to look after the captain's mate. It was terribly hot on board the burning ship, almost impossible to be there, but we carried the mate down into the salon so that he could go down with the ship. Then we took some food and clothing. I burned my feet quite a bit, as I didn't have any shoes on.

Haslund. Then you took yourselves off?

Larsen. No, first we got hold of a little four-oared boat which had not been damaged. Then we separated into two groups for the two boats and rigged up sails on both. After we had sailed all forenoon, we were picked up by an English destroyer. She was one of a unit of four and we were on board for six days.

Haslund. Did anything happen while you were there?

Larsen. Yes, I think they got seven German submarines all told. The one I was aboard got two. When they picked them up with the detector, they dropped seven or eight depth charges, which made considerable noise. The submarine was thrown upwards with terrific force to within about a fathom of the surface, so we saw her quite clearly. And then she sank like a rock. Once they got a big whale, too. With the detector it is probably difficult to hear the difference between a submarine and a whale, but we saw the difference when it came up. The destroyer, by the way, went back to the burning wreck and tried to sink it with cannon fire. But the lumber cargo kept it afloat and it didn't sink until all of it had been burned up.

Haslund. You weren't in a convoy, then, when you were attacked?

Larsen. No, we went over alone that time. But while we were on the destroyer, we got an SOS from a convoy about forty miles away. All the destroyers dashed off, and none of the ships in the convoy were sunk; only one was slightly damaged.

Haslund. Were you set ashore in England?

Larsen. Yes, we came to a shipping port and were signed off there.

Haslund. Finally, Larsen, there is a question I should like to ask you. Answer me frankly, without regard to the fact that we are on the air. Have you, during all these experiences, seen many of your comrades become hysterical or lose their self-control?

Larsen. That I can tell you quite frankly. I have seen one man. His nerves couldn't stand it. But otherwise, I don't think we Norwegian seamen have a tendency to display our emotions to any great extent or to lose our self-control. Seafarers have become by degrees a kind of people used to facing difficult situations and mastering them.

(This radio interview is one of a series which Mr. Haslund, Secretary of the Welfare Committee for Norwegian Sailors, held with the men. It was also Mr. Haslund who directed the transport of gold out of Norway during the occupation.)

The North Atlantic

8

Convoy

BY NORDAHL GRIEG

The first day on board, before we put out into the North Atlantic from a west English port, we had lifeboat drill. It was a singular experience. I was in the mate's boat and the row maneuver lasted about five minutes. The words this spirited young mate used to urge us on at the oars the day before we were to go into the danger zone gave one the feeling of sitting in a yellow wherry on a peaceful Norwegian fjord—as if many, many years had passed and the war was so unreal and far away it could be joked about.

"Hang on, boys," he shouted. "Land's in sight! Hang on!" And under other, similar commands we made our one trip around the boat.

That same evening I saw him standing on the bridge, blond forelock under a steel helmet, machine gun in hand and shooting at a German bomber. The sky ceiling was low and the planes flew pretty high, but off and on a dark shadow droned over our heads. Then the mate let go a round of glowing tracer bullets into the misty gloom.

"It's great to have the tools," he explained. He gave the impression of running a winch or doing some other normal ship work. The skipper stood beside him, bareheaded, his hands in the pockets of his oilskins, watching him with interest and fatherly good will.

In the gray of dawn we weighed anchor and stood off, in the captain's words, "to meet the convoy out in the meadows."

Presently the ships had fallen into rows and lines, and in a slow plod we began our trip across the ocean. We would be in dangerous waters for eight days or thereabouts, where much could happen and had already happened.

A watch stood by the large yellow-painted cannon on the poop all day. We did not undress at night. The helmsman and lookout had life belts on. I walked about constantly with a bulging, downy blue puff bound around my chest, looking like some sort of eider duck. The captain and the mates wore swimming vests deflated and elegant under their jackets; when they sat down to eat, a rubber tube with a nickeled nozzle would pop out at the shoulder, making them look momentarily like patients with cancer of the throat. We were well protected by eight naval vessels, destroyers, corvettes, and armed trawlers. Every day during the first week we had seaplanes above us. Night was the time of uncertainty: under darkness U-boats might sneak up from astern.

What was the nature of life on board this Norwegian ship during the evenings and nights in the danger zone? After the evening meal I went into one of the cabins on the seamen's side. A man stood painting. It was a very large picture he was working on. It portrayed an elk with lifelike realism, the elk snorting against a blood-red background. The painter had a stack of other canvases under his bunk. His cabin mate, who lay smoking, jumped down and pulled them out. They were of white passenger ships in blue seas against green palm islands, and female figures in chaste silver-gray tones. But for the moment he had the urge to express something about this elk he had not yet been able to say.

Apart from having solved his own personal problem by

self-imposed activity, this man, more than any other, had been instrumental in providing everyone on the ship with something to think about. It was he who had brought the cat on board, which everyone now adopted as his own. There was already a dog on board—what's more, the skipper's. Everything was therefore set for absorbing conflicts.

The dog was an elkhound from Norway. The moment he heard child voices on the radio, far-off memories came to life and he leaped up, ready for play. Otherwise, from morning to night he had his paws all set for attention to duties. Outraged in his innermost soul because the sea gulls alighted on the mast tops, he must pursue these audacious fellows; he must crouch on the deck ready to frighten away the destroyers that in such an irritating way intruded upon his personal watch; he must growl threateningly at some of the sailors who had perhaps on the sly smacked him on the snout with a sharp sou'ester when he barked at them. Furthermore, it was his heavy duty between times to race aft to discipline the cat.

The cat was skinny, yellow, had a miserably small head suggestive of a sapped herring. She was a harbor cat, a war cat. The elk painter had seen her one day among the ruins in an English port town; she had followed trustingly after him. An air raid had come, and two hours later when he stepped out of a shelter the cat stood waiting for him. He took her on board. Everyone aft was fond of her; she leaped through the bull's-eyes and into their bunks and lay beside them purring.

Now and then she missed a male companion and voiced her complaint. Her friend the painter had tried to find a cat in England that could keep her company.

"But you just wait," he said to me with fanatical zeal, "when we get to New York I'll provide her with a real American—"

Whenever the dog came dashing along determined on a

settlement, it might happen that the cat would jump up on the poop and eye her enemy with watchful hatred until the dog grew tired of barking and turned back triumphant. But as a rule she flew straight into his face wild and spitting, and put him to flight. Then the crew was jubilant, and the cat became a sports hero, an unbeatable Birger Ruud whom they honored at the homecoming. On such occasions it was rumored that the cat trained on raw meat. She refused to drink canned milk lest she lose some of her savagery.

In the cabin next to the elk painter's was a young able-bodied seaman. He had been on the ship a long time and therefore had many kinds of decorations around his bunk: a silk coverlet with an embroidered golden tiger from Japan on it; a woolen rug with kneeling camels from Suez; a girl from Sandefjord artfully framed in a red heart. He was reading. It was a much-used book. Curiously enough it had once belonged to Anthon B. Nilsen, and was the *Spanish Textbook for Beginners* by Kristoffer Nyrop. It was open to page 49. I read: "Dá muchas expressiones a tu hermana," etc. In translation: "Greet your sister many times and tell her that she owes me a waltz at the first ball where we meet." "I shall not fail to do so." "Good night, sir, sleep well."

The young student of Spanish kindly showed me his collection of amateur snapshots. They were from exotic places interspersed with pictures from a bicycle tour in Numedal. Like a whimsical song with a haunting, ever-recurring refrain I heard him relate: "This is from Curaçao . . . that is from Yokohama . . . that is from home . . . that is from Aberdeen . . . that is from Sydney . . . that is from Swansea . . . that is from home . . . that is from Cape Town . . . that is from Suez . . . that is from Gibraltar . . . that is from home."

His companion in the other cabin bunk was a sailor from Haugesund. He was in his thirties. He lay motionless on his back and gazed up at the ceiling. On the bulkhead hung a picture of himself and his wife on board a ship. He turned toward me: "That was taken in Rouen. I was bosun aboard there. I had my wife with me for three months. I came from that ship when I signed on here. They were good folk."

"Was it torpedoed?" I asked.

He nodded. "I was wounded," he exclaimed.

He showed me a wound—a bloody fresh scar in a net of stitches that covered his whole left shoulder. A German plane —the largest he had seen in his life—with eight Gatling guns and two machine guns had attacked the ship. He was running up the companionway to the reinforced concrete lookout on the bridge when he was hit. Then he fainted. But the gunner on board, a Canadian, "was a plucky one—he stayed at the machine gun and kept firing, completely unprotected; at last he shot down the plane." The sailor had come here directly from the hospital and had not told anyone he had been wounded, until now.

In other cabins the men played gramophones, smoked or read. Pictures of the family at home always hung on the bulkheads, and not infrequently the photograph of a Norwegian youngster standing in the snow or by a garden gate which bore the name of a firm in some unlooked-for city— Curaçao or Sydney. They were amateur snapshots that had been enlarged. The father could not come home, but the child seemed nearer to him by being made larger—almost grew before his eyes during this time when he was not permitted to see him grow.

The worst place on board a ship in the danger zone is undoubtedly the engine room. Those down there have so many ladders to run up; they can see nothing; they stand half naked in the heat; outside a bone-chilling storm may be raging. I went down to the white-painted, majestic engine room where gleaming pistons worked in the still, oily air. Since the donkeyman was from Bergen, my own town, I immedi-

ately asked what he thought of being on the North Atlantic
in these times. He didn't answer the question—but he said
in our melancholy dialect: "It's got better in lots of ways
since the war started. I can now smoke when I please here
in the engine room and it's nobody's business."

I went on deck again and up forward. It was pitch dark.
The streets of London in the blackout are a sea of light compared with a ship in blackout on the North Atlantic. Not the
faintest light may show.

In the passageway I met the mate. "These will be anxious
days," he said. I looked at him, astonished that he was so
communicative. "Yes, the way things are going in Egypt," he
clarified.

From the third mate's quarters came the strains of a
violin. By a self-instruction system the mate was busy teaching
himself the sixth position on the neck of the violin.

The door of the steward's cabin was open. He sat meek
and helpless on a chair with a towel around his neck. He was
having his hair cut by the pantry boy. There had been this
and that to do while they were lying close to land; now it was
time to tidy up a bit.

Up on the bridge I fell into conversation with the second
mate. We talked about summers at home. Once he had taken
a long motorboat trip with his wife down along the Swedish
coast. For dinner they had had fish which they themselves
had caught and good butter and new potatoes. We began to
talk about Sweden.

"I like Sweden very much," he mused. "When we reached
Strömstad, there along the pier—and it was as long as this
ship—lay a line of Norwegian motorboats crowded together
as close as they could be and all with Norwegian flags. Sweden
is a fine country to travel in."

The captain came out on the bridge for a turn. His berth
had been untouched for eight days. He spent most of his time

beside the wheelhouse or in the chartroom. Often one found him alone down in his own quarters seated in a leather chair reading a book, or he was playing chess. He was always friendly and at ease. It was as if he had a surfeit of time now that he had left off sleeping. He had watched over this ship while she was being built and had been on board her ever since. Others could sign off and get a rest ashore; never he. He was responsible for the ship; his only thought was to bring her safely home again.

"Experience proves," he said one night, "that torpedoed ships are often abandoned before it is necessary. That is foolish. Perhaps the ship can be saved. At any rate you can stay aboard for a while, eat, smoke, and take your ease. The lifeboat is not so comfortable that you have to rush into it."

The radio operator came out on the bridge with a message. The waters to westward were not clear of U-boats. Well, there was nothing to do about that.

The young seaman who was studying Spanish came up on the bridge to take his turn at the wheel. His companion went out from the wheelhouse and found the second mate in the dark. "Keep her just as she is." "Aye, aye, just as she is."

Behind the shoulder-high reinforced concrete wall I saw the able-bodied seaman's face in the dim sheen of the compass. What was he thinking about? Perhaps he was practicing his Spanish exercises; perhaps he was conversing with the unknown foe who lay in wait for us somewhere out in the sea.

"Buenas noches, señor, duerme bien."

"Good night, sir, sleep well."

While we sat at supper on our fourth night at sea, a crash resounded beside the ship with such a bang as to make the whole bulkhead tremble. The skipper performed to perfection the double duty expected of him—calmly finished chewing the piece of sausage in his mouth and at the same time disappeared up the ladder to the bridge with the utmost rapidity.

A short distance off our port three destroyers had formed a ring. A fourth raced into the circle and dropped depth bombs; we saw the column of water spout skyward, and the bang followed quickly. The three naval vessels lay listening and alert. Suddenly they let out faint swift signal flashes. The task was done and there was one U-boat less. The destroyers hurried back again into place through the darkening sea, their bows buried in spray; the sunlight slanted from the western sky's icy blue between violet cloud banks.

The next evening there was another crash. It undoubtedly meant that one more U-boat had been tracked down and destroyed. The following morning a flying boat appeared from so far out on the horizon that it looked like a floating pencil. All of a sudden it dived and loosed a bomb. It circled low over the spot, and then came the Morse flashes to the lead ship. We read them to mean that this was the third.

One place on board where it was always good to be was the radio operator's room. Like the wheelhouse and charthouse it was protected with extra walls and ceiling of heavy concrete. In this windowless hollow sat Sparks in a blue sweater under the green-shaded work lamp, always genial and considerate, his pipe in his mouth and the red box of Prince Albert tobacco within reach.

We listened to the short-wave broadcast from Berlin. The news was preceded by a number of double strokes on a bell, each clang supposed to symbolize a sunken ship.

The idea was taken from Lloyd's of London, where a vessel stricken from the registry was announced by a single clang of the bell in the hall. The Germans might seem to have hit upon an excellent propaganda idea: to let the death knell for the lost ships toll out over the ocean to be heard in the darkness of the night by other vessels in the same dangerous waters as a warning of their own inevitable fate, to break their will and courage. But the very fact that the radio operator, philosophically smoking his pipe, should turn his radio on at all and dial to find the broadcast showed how futile the German scheme was. His own quiet calm transformed the bells of terror into something melodramatic and hysterical; this was not the language in which to speak to him. The more bell strokes there were—one night there were twenty-two— the stronger grew the feeling of the childishness of the fright device. It was a kind of meeting between two men, the one in Berlin who in triumphant irritation danged the bell, the other on board the Norwegian ship who interestedly and with head shakings studied his opponent. When he switched off the radio, he had been strengthened for the struggle. He didn't take to noisy people.

We listened, of course, chiefly to Norwegian news broadcasts from Boston. The voices were well liked; a lively personal interest surrounded the persons behind the voices. The woman who read the news was welcomed into this womanless world as if she were some extraordinary guest; it was as if somebody they could not have hoped to see had come on a delightful surprise visit: wife, daughter, mother.

When our national anthem was played at the close of the program, we stood. Never have I known this song to be more moving than in this half-darkened radio room on the tossing Atlantic. It evoked not only the first sighting of that land we love so well; we stood assuredly at the pure, fierce fountainhead of the song, as Nordraak and Björnson created it in their pledge to fight for freedom.

Otherwise, it is my belief that on board Norwegian ships they prefer to avoid big feelings—at any rate, big words. I am reminded of a scene from the greatest sea novel ever written, *Typhoon* by Joseph Conrad. A sailor has been at the wheel in the wild, terrifying storm for twenty-four hours and longer; he has the ship so well in hand that the skipper would like him to continue. He asks the pale, dogged man, who has not uttered a single word the whole time he has stood there, if he thinks he can keep on. "By heavens, sir, I can steer forever if you don't talk to me."

In silence the seamen go about their work. What they want is to have the best possible protection, the best possible conditions in their hard, danger-filled lives. "Give us the tools, and the job will be done." They know better than anyone else that the job must be done. They have stood and are standing in the front line of the fight against Nazism, against the fermenting putrefaction of brutality and impotence that spawn new wars every twenty years.

Then came the day when we were released from the convoy. The skipper was overjoyed when we could push off and be on our own, while the ships spread over the sea. To have to move in pitch darkness, or still worse in fog, with the certainty that the waters swarmed with invisible ships, forward, astern, to port and starboard, struck at the very foundation of what he conceived to be seamanlike responsibility. He would regard being torpedoed while alone at sea as a war casualty; but collision under convoy would be a misfortune that touched him much deeper personally.

We zigzagged for several days. We began to undress at night; soon we held a steady course. We were in safe waters, and the days suddenly seemed longer.

Now and then we met eastbound convoys. With masts and smoking stacks against the gray ocean air they resembled dark industrial towns on the move; a warship rose like an Eiffel Tower high above the factories.

We were stopped a few times by warships. "Who are you?" We ran up signals for identification, and the questioner blinked: "W A Y, good voyage," and we answered: "O V F, thanks."

Through waves of northern lights, snowstorms, or calm phosphorescent nights we had come far westward. Now we no longer heard the Boston broadcast in the evening but in the broad light of afternoon, with Sparks sitting not in a sweater but in a singlet. Suddenly we were in the Gulf Stream, a blue summer lapped gently around the ship, brown Florida seaweed drifted past the sides, and it was difficult to pull in the log. Small jellyfish—Portuguese men-of-war—rushed off, borne along by their white half-moon-shaped sails. They resembled parachute troops from some elfin war on the sea. All over the deck, clotheslines were run up, and fresh, clean underwear flapped in the sunshine. We neared land.

One morning I was up at four o'clock to be on deck when the American coast hove into sight. It was late in the afternoon before I saw the sea gulls (we had watched for them so long) cast their great gliding shadows in dark splotches on the masonry of Manhattan's skyscrapers.

9

A Freighter Fights a Submarine

That this ship is afloat must actually be called a miracle. I have never seen the likes of it. She was hit not once or twice but a thousand times, and the holes are not small either. Some shells pierced four or five metal plates before stopping. The radio room was smashed to pieces by three or four direct hits, putting the radio out of commission. Fortunately, the telegrapher was out on deck when this happened. What he got was a whole cascade of splinters in both legs and one foot. Several cabins were riddled by shells, and the cook can thank his lucky stars that he wasn't in his cabin. His bed is full of splinters and the walls are in ruins. The bridge is punctured with holes; the foredeck has a hole big enough for a man to fall through. The ammunition depot is gone; it burned down completely as shell after shell exploded. And in spite of all this, only one man was killed and two were wounded. The rest are in the best of health and working vigorously as I pay them this early Monday-morning visit. An acrid stench of blood hangs in the air, but it comes from the Brazilian hides which are being unloaded.

Even from the pier you can see big holes in the ship's side, fortunately *above* the waterline. On board you cannot take two steps without seeing new evidence of the life-and-death battle fought out on it "somewhere in the Atlantic" last Thursday morning. The cabin of the skipper is relatively undamaged except for the water pipe, which is out of order, and the electricity, which is now being restored. The stern is badly damaged; the members of the crew who had their cabins there lost practically everything they owned. But their lives are safe, and so are their good spirits, it seems.

Captain Hans Nielsen, who comes from Vasser on the Oslo Fjord, just chanced to be the skipper on this trip. Ordinarily it would have been Captain Anders Nielsen, his brother. Captain Hans is a man in his fifties, big as a bear, energetic, sun-tanned, with eyes that look pale in their gypsy-brown setting. He laughs as he tells his story—somehow he can't get over the fact that he is actually *here* in New York harbor. "The steward shakes his head every time he sees me," he says, "and tells me he doesn't understand how I managed to come through. As a matter of fact *I* didn't do anything except smoke and curse because we didn't have a bigger cannon so we could make an end of the beast. I was of course on the bridge all the time, and was standing right beside the telegrapher when he was wounded; there were splinters everywhere, and I didn't get as much as a scratch! I must say the crew was wonderful."

The crew, a bit international, consisted of one Swede, one Finn, two Danes, an American, a Portuguese, a Brazilian, and twenty-five Norwegians.

The fight took place sometime during the night between Wednesday and Thursday. "All of a sudden," says the captain, "an enormous spinning fireball appeared in the sky about seven or eight nautical miles off port side. Our instant thought was that some U-boat had sent a decoy, since the thing didn't resemble a rocket—just another one of their little tricks. So off we started full speed in the opposite direction. The U-boat had in all probability taken our bearings through her listening apparatus."

At five o'clock in the morning, just at dawn, the skipper

was warned by the first mate that he was watching something which resembled a U-boat. All hands were ordered out and the speed was ordered under forced draft. They didn't want to start shooting, however, since they didn't feel sure; it might be a motorboat. But the U-boat lost no time in displaying her flag and began firing from a distance of between two and two and a half nautical miles. Sparks had just managed to send an SOS, but before the position could be indicated, the transmitter was already out of commission. He turned to the emergency transmitter, but it too had been blasted to pieces. Then Sparks came on deck, only to be struck himself, though he had somehow managed to get down to the salon on his own. "I have never seen the likes of that boy for coolness," says the captain. Sparks stood beside the boatswain when he was struck by one of the first volleys and killed instantly. The U-boat kept up an incessant barrage and many of the men were bowled over by the air pressure. Several of the crew are still suffering from deafness. One hit demolished the chartroom.

The captain continues: "Most of the hits struck aft, particularly on the cannon platform. We kept shooting back all the time and by shifting our course got the submarine directly astern at such an angle as to give her as small a target as possible. Then we set our course right against the sun in order to dazzle the sub crew.

"It would be unfair to single out any one of the men, for all of them were brilliant. Nonetheless, I must be permitted to say that the gunner, who of course stands in a special position inasmuch as he is the only military personage on board, was absolutely fabulous. He is a twenty-year-old boy from Florö, Sverre B. He sent out fourteen blasts and says himself that he is certain he scored at least one hit. When he stopped firing, I tried to telephone across to him, but the wire had been broken. Then I shouted and he answered that he had no more ammuition on the platform and that the magazine was on fire. The Germans continued shooting. The deck was strewn with splinters having German names and even swastikas on them. The mate gave orders to extinguish the fire, but the waterpipe was broken. Then we tried carbon dioxide, the gas extinguisher, which was kept aft in a little house by itself, but there were no tubes from there down to the poop. Everybody set to work to stop the fire; we unfastened the extinguishers, carried them across the deck and unscrewed the plugs, then threw them down on the iron plates, already glowing red. In the magazine one shell after the other was exploding, and two men went right down into it to extinguish the fire. They were an American machinist and the third mate, a Dane.

"After about twenty minutes the Germans stopped shooting and moved over to port side. We then changed to starboard to keep them right aft. The situation was serious because they began gaining on us, and with our engine damaged we couldn't make full speed.

"At this critical moment we saw smoke on the horizon and heard the drone of airplane engines! I'll tell you the submarine disappeared in a hurry. The American patrols must have heard the cannonade, for we never had time to send any SOS. We couldn't follow closely what did happen because the smoke was too thick, but in a little while an American destroyer drew alongside us and gave the position. The airplane circled above us and then a blimp came sailing in and that gave us an escort that availed. The blimp came quite close to us twice, so I could stand on the bridge and talk to the pilot without the aid of any mechanical device.

"A doctor came aboard from the destroyer to bandage our two wounded men. They were then transferred to the destroyer, which had better facilities for taking care of them. I'll never forget that young Danish telegrapher as he lay smiling at us from the bottom of the boat which transported him. That's what I call a real man!

"The fire was still raging and the destroyer offered us a transportable pump; she also offered to tow us in, but we declined the offer with thanks. We did, however, ask to have an escort to shore. After a few hours we had trouble with the steering gear: the telemotor tube was burned off. We tried the manual steering apparatus, but that was too hot and was developing so much gas that we had to give it up. After a long time we got the fire extinguished and the steering gear working again. Before long the engine stalled again; this time it was a shell splinter in a packing box. The chief engineer, who is always very cool-headed, came to tell us what the trouble was but added that he thought he could put the engine in working order again. He managed it all right and we could almost get up full speed. Meanwhile the destroyer kept signaling that there were U-boats around and the blimp flashed lights on the spot where it thought the U-boat was and the destroyer dropped depth bombs. So there certainly was a hell of a racket. Late that night we reached port."

The reception in New York was great and enthusiastic. Admiral Adolphus Andrews invited the captain to his quarters and was very much interested in hearing the details. The big New York papers carried long articles on the event. It is an example of what close inter-Allied co-operation can lead to. Moreover, the incident had the happy ending too often lacking in modern tales of the sea.

The skipper of course emphasizes that they only did their plain duty as Norwegian seamen, and does not seem able to get over the fact that he is alive! "But I must confess it is rather nice," he says in his broad east-country dialect, a refreshing variation from the more commonly heard and softer dialects.

A tour of the ship, now in dock in Brooklyn directly

across from the Battery in Manhattan, almost makes one doubt one's own senses. The lifeboats are riddled with holes, the rafts are inutile, and the ventilators slant pathetically. But activity is in full swing—crews are loading, adjusters are estimating damage, friends and colleagues are offering congratulations, journalists and radio commentators are pressing for information, the telephone rings incessantly.

On the cannon platform the young naval gunner is quietly and carefully oiling the dear old cannon which did such a good job. It is a beautiful picture: the blond, almost towheaded, sun-tanned boy beside his precious gun, against the background of a busy harbor, ferries on their way to the island, the Statue of Liberty, and the almost ethereal skyline of Manhattan rising high into the air. Though the gunner is a man of few words, it was possible to draw a couple of facts from him. He took part in the war in Norway, did service on the S.S. *Heimdal,* crossed to England, where he went through gunner's school, and had now been at work as a gunner on Norwegian ships for a year and a half, always in the danger zone. "But I have always had luck: I was never torpedoed," he adds with finality.

Five or six boys stand around, all young, blond, and looking alike. Had anything in the experience made a special impression on them? No, nothing in particular. Everybody had been entirely all right. Then they began talking about the boatswain, who was killed. He had been the representative of the Association of Seamen aboard the ship. His name was Jon Saetre; he hailed from Haugesund and was a man of about forty. He had been a quiet, solid sort of man and a good friend. A few hours from now he would be buried from the Seamen's Church. One could see that the thought weighed heavily on the young minds.

On my way to the newspaper office I passed the Norwegian Hospital and stopped by to see the telegrapher whom they had all talked about—the Dane who smiled and waved to his comrades when he was being carried aboard the destroyer. He was a Faeroese by the name of Hans Mortensen and had been sailing for three years as a telegrapher. His leg was injured seriously, but the people at the hospital said that no one had ever heard a sound of pain from him. He had just come from Brazil, where he was laid up on a Danish ship in Santos for two years. The Danish ship had now been requisitioned by the Brazilian government. He had spent only eighteen days on this Norwegian ship but says he likes being on a Norwegian vessel. What impressed him most during the fight? That would probably have to be the helmsman, who went on steering all the while with shells screeching to right and left of his head. No nervousness noticeable in that fellow. And the skipper had been as cool as a cake of ice.

An exceptionally fine spirit dominated this ship—you noticed it immediately. Everyone emphasized the job done by the man who lay next to him. The young Danish third mate, Thorvald Knudsen, said: "If we cannot sail under our own flag, we have to sail under other flags. The main thing is to get the sailing done."

10

A Norwegian Whaler in Action:
The "Kosmos II" Chases a U-Boat

From the New York Daily News, February 7, 1942

Some U-boat commander out in the deep Atlantic would in all probability choke on his hunk of *knackwurst* if he could read this story. For it tells how a Norwegian whale factory-ship, without as much as a single BB cannon on board, chased a submarine and would have rammed it if it could have made a couple of knots more speed.

The sub fled. The commander obviously believed that he was being chased by a big battleship or in any event by an armored merchant ship. The report of this pursuit is this war's first example of how a U-boat will zigzag like crazy to escape a defenseless whaling vessel.

Captain Einar Gleditsch, the hero of this story, is thirty-six years old and has been on board whaling vessels since he was a youngster. His ship is the whaler *Kosmos II*, a huge 25,410-tonner now in use by the Norwegian Shipping and Trade Mission in conjunction with the British Admiralty. The U-boat chase occurred January 19, 1942.

At 6:00 A.M. the *Kosmos II* was working its way along Cape Hatteras. Suddenly the automatic wireless alarm rang in

Captain Gleditsch's cabin, warning that an SOS signal had been received. The signal indicated a distress call from a ship attacked by a U-boat.

"The vessel sending the signal lay between us and the coast," said the captain. "We have strict orders not to help any ship attacked by a U-boat, so I set my course away from the coast and ordered the mate to put on full speed."

A couple of minutes later one of the officers on the bridge signaled that the wake of the sub was seen at starboard. This was enough for Captain Gleditsch. He followed orders and steered away. But if these U-boats were eager for some sport he was game.

He gave orders for a course calculated to cut across that of the sub. "We weren't fooling now. I gave the engineer orders to sink it. We could just make it out with its periscope sticking up out of the water. Finally we were within a couple hundred feet of it. It must have thought we were well-armed. First it tried to submerge; then it surfaced and began zig-zagging with its periscope two feet above the water. A little later it settled into a steady course and we pursued it for about forty-five minutes."

Captain Gleditsch's only explanation as to why the U-boat didn't deliver any torpedoes was that it probably didn't have any left or that it didn't have any stern-mounted torpedo tube. He laughed. "Had they only known that we were unarmored they could have blown us to bits with their big deck cannons. We could see it surfacing for long periods at a time." And the skipper said, stirred: "If only we could have made another knot or two faster speed. You see we have a re-inforced bow, something which is very useful when we are out whaling and have to break through ice. It would also have been useful for cutting U-boats in two. Had we been able to overtake this fellow, it would have been the end of him."

After a forty-five-minute pursuit the U-boat had got too

far away and the *Kosmos II* gave up. Captain Gleditsch radioed the station on shore and it sent out planes. He himself resumed his course, but added, "I should have liked to chase that parasite right into Berlin."

Addendum on *Kosmos II:* "I have heard on good authority that a whale floating factory-ship, namely, *Kosmos II,* was torpedoed en route from New York to England. I do not know whether the cargo that time was whale oil, petrol, or something else. At any rate it did have a number of Greeks on board who were bound for Europe to take part in the war. I believe this was in 1942. The factory was traveling in convoy when it was hit by a torpedo. Panic rose, or an approach to it among the 'passengers.' Meanwhile the factory continued to float and could also move on its own power. The Greeks were put on board another ship, while *Kosmos II* was to continue with its own crew. It could not, however, keep pace with the convoy and was torpedoed a second time (the following day?) and sank. The crew was picked up by other ships. All the same some of them happened to get on a ship which was also to be torpedoed. Thus he [Captain Gleditsch] was torpedoed three times on the one trip."*

* From a letter to me received during the winter of 1967. This information on the fate of *Kosmos II* was fortuitously included in answer to my general questions concerning whale factory-ships.—*N.O.S.*

11

Four Lifeboats Adrift

Forty-seven men in four Norwegian lifeboats drifted in the
Atlantic in a bad April storm, no boat for less than ten days.
They were the survivors of the two ships the M.S. *Koll* and
the M.S. *Kollskjegg,* both torpedoed on the same day in
early April. The loss of life had been small: three men in
all. Two of them had been killed by the explosion; the third
had died at sea of cold and exposure. All the boats reached
safety; one of them reached land by itself. The lifeboat is
the hero.

—From the daybook of KARSTEN IDZAR

Eight men of the 15,000-ton tanker *Koll* were hospitalized
for a few days at the Norwegian Hospital in Brooklyn, a hospital which has proved a godsend to many shipwrecked sailors
during the first trying days after a rescue. By request these
eight were all in the same ward. Some had suffered frozen
hands or feet, but none had been seriously wounded. All were
blue-eyed, tanned, full of sunshine and optimism.

Second Mate Karsten Idzar knows how to get around the
difficulty of describing a torpedoing, even though it does happen so fast. He asked me to glance through his little black,
leather-covered 1940 daybook, which he had used as a kind of
personal logbook. It seems to have followed him through many
countries and latitudes, with addresses of the Norwegian

Mates' Association in Glasgow, a Norwegian dentist in Brooklyn, the Seamen's Church in Buenos Aires. It says:

"On Monday, April 6, 1942 (Easter Monday), a violent explosion occurred aft on the port side. The *Koll* had been torpedoed, and the torpedo had probably struck just in front of the engine where the oil tank was. The tank exploded and immediately a column of flaming oil shot up higher than the mast, and fire and smoke almost reached midship. From the bridge it looked as if the whole stern had been demolished. The ship began sinking and the motorboat was lowered to the water. Waves partly extinguished the fire where it had reached the deck. The men came running from aft, swung out the starboard lifeboat and managed to get clear of the sinking ship. The submarine surfaced and asked the name of our ship. We got the impression that the sub was Italian.

"*Koll*'s bow now stood perpendicular to the sky with water reaching the front mast; but she did not sink. The sub started shooting incendiary shells at her and hit tank number 1. Oil started burning. A violent explosion followed and the *Koll* disappeared sometime between 11:00 and 11:15 A.M. We counted men. Three were missing and we started searching for them. A Canadian was in the sea, doing rather well under the circumstances. He had managed to get hold of a raft, but it had drifted right into the flames, so he had jumped overboard and was just swimming around. The weather was pleasant, and the latitude being southerly, the salt water did him hardly any damage for several hours."

Not all hands were saved, however. "First Engineer Einar Gulbrandsen, 45, of Arendal, and the motorman Johannes Tjöne, 25, of Kristianssund were missing. It is a miracle that so many were saved. I don't understand how all the men aft managed to escape the flames.

"All of us put on oilskins, which proved very useful. Unfortunately there were no wool stockings in the lifeboat, and that lack almost made cripples of some of the men.

"We called a short council of war and decided to try to reach the East Coast of the United States north of Cape Hatteras. The motorboat with the captain on board tried towing the two other boats. And we hoisted sail to help increase the speed with a course NW.

"*April 7*. Towed all night. In the morning a wind blew up, and we had to go on by ourselves. We kept sight of the motorboat for about three hours but then we had a stiff breeze from about 10:00 A.M. to 4:00 P.M. We met a lifeboat from the M.S. *Kollskjegg*, another ship belonging to our line. She had been torpedoed at almost the same time as ours. We tried to speak to the men but could not get close enough because of the wind, rain, and heavy sea. But we managed to give them the position and our course. We soon lost sight of them. On the following day we lost contact with our other lifeboat, where the first mate was in charge. Until then we had been able to keep together. We had agreed that the first boat to receive assistance was to report concerning the other two.

"The weather was bad. The breeze had stiffened, the sea was heavy. We were in the middle of a tempest. The wind stopped and waves washed over us from everywhere. We used an oar to keep the stern against the breaking seas and had to bail water out of the boat constantly. Violent rainfalls quieted the sea. The next day we were able to set sail again. The Spaniard Anido had an aching foot all the time, but he was able nevertheless to control the rudder and to help in other ways. Erick, who from the very start had complained of pains in his hip, was now quite helpless. Everyone began having pains in his feet and legs.

"*April 10*. We came into the Labrador Current at about 11:00 A.M. It was terribly cold, but we stuck to our course. We had been drenched ever since we got into the lifeboats and were all suffering from the cold.

"*April 11*. The night was bitterly cold; everybody suffered, and it was particularly hard on the legs. At about 2:00 P.M. we noticed that we were in the Gulf Stream again. Wind and current had driven us far from shore. We decided to go southward into warmer waters, for everybody was frozen with cold and our legs were getting very bad. Storm blasts shifted from north to west. The waves grew bigger with heavy vaulting crests, but the boat proved to be excellently seaworthy. The storm raged through the night, but the boat filled with water only once, and we were able to bail it out immediately. We decided to keep on going all night. The next night it was better.

"*April 14.* Sun and fine weather; we could set all sails. We shed our oilskins and dried our underwear. Most of us had inflamed feet. We washed them with salt water and rubbed them with oil but they ached badly.

"On April 15 at 4:00 A.M. the watchman saw a light on the horizon. We sent up two rockets at a five-minute interval. Since it looked as if they noticed us, we sent up a third rocket. Just as dawn broke, a fully illuminated freighter came right towards our lifeboat. It was a Swiss vessel, the S.S. *Gerque.* She took all of us on board and gave us the very best of care. The second mate had had some medical training and treated everyone. He said we had been rescued at the very last moment, as several of us would have had to have our feet amputated if it had lasted a few days or even hours longer. To our delight the ship was bound for New York. We wanted to go there."

The other boys in the room, who had been listening with interest and enthusiasm, went on exclaiming about the Swiss ship. Being on it was exactly like sailing in peacetime with full lights, they said. And the treatment could not have been better! They were also full of praises for the Norwegian Hospital in Brooklyn. None of them would ask for another thing—they were simply given everything here.

What everyone returned to constantly in the conversation

was their wonderful lifeboat. It had been altogether seaworthy and was excellently equipped. These, for example, had been their daily rations: Breakfast: two white biscuits with corned beef, two or three oatmeal biscuits, three milk tablets, two chocolate tablets, one cup of water with milk. Lunch: two white biscuits, two oatmeal biscuits, three milk tablets, one chocolate tablet, pemmican, and one cup of water. Dinner: two white biscuits, two oatmeal biscuits, three milk tablets, two chocolate tablets, and water. Nobody suffered from hunger, but during the last days they were thirsty and the water ration was given out in the evening and sometimes at night. After nine days at sea they still had rations for more than a fortnight in the boat.

The second mate of the *Koll*, Karsten Idzar, wanted especially to emphasize that everyone put on a brave face and that the spirits of the crew were fine all the time. Looking at these eager, weather-beaten young figures, one could hardly doubt the claim. But they were still anxious about their comrades in the other lifeboats. They hadn't much hope; the weather was so bad all the time.

Half an hour later all of them were smiling broadly: a telephone message had just come from Nortraship that the lifeboat of the first mate had reached shore, all hands safe. All they needed now was a message from the motorboat and the captain!

A week later I happened to pass the hospital and went in again to see the boys. Happily I did not know many; most of those who had been there the week before had checked out. In the bed where Second Mate Karsten Idzar had been I now found First Mate Arne Tvedt, also of the *Koll*. He gave me the happy news that the third lifeboat, the motorboat in charge of the captain, had been rescued by a ship bound for Portugal. Everyone was O.K. He had another piece of news too: the lifeboat from the *Kollskjegg*, which they sighted drifting in the sea but afterward lost, had arrived safely in Florida. "They're not bad, those lifeboats," first mate Tvedt remarked calmly.

He went on to tell about the experiences in *his* lifeboat. The U-boat had thrown out two boxes of biscuits with the name Hamburg printed on them. Had the sub been German after all? Or had the Italians just received some help from big brother? On the third day the lifeboats lost sight of each other, and "we sailed before full sails," said the first mate smilingly. They spent ten days in the lifeboat, three of them on drag anchor. They protected themselves against the heavy sea by tying oars and empty breadboxes together. The weather was very bad. During the night of April 14 the steward, Sigurd Askeland of Bergen, died of cold and exposure. They buried him in the sea at sunset the next day.

Finally at dawn on the tenth day they sighted the masts of a ship just above the horizon. They sent up a flare and the ship immediately changed course and came to the rescue. It was a small Portuguese freighter bound for the United States. The shipwrecked Norwegians got excellent treatment. The ship had a male nurse on board, which was fortunate, for the second engineer was very badly burned and had suffered terrible pains in the lifeboat. "In the lifeboat we hardly dared stir from our places for fear of touching and hurting him," said the first mate.

The crew was put ashore somewhere in Delaware; and the second engineer was brought to the nearest hospital and was recovering very well.

12

A Ten-Day Battle for Survival in a Storm

BY ADAM EGEDE-NISSEN

January 1942

Our ship has been traveling alone for many days—the convoy was broken up shortly after we left Iceland. The captain has said, "We will be in New York in three days."

January 17. Evening. Pitch dark. The sea has calmed somewhat and the 11,000-tonner is gliding more smoothly through the waves. We two passengers are sitting at the table down in the steward's pantry drinking coffee and talking about what we will do when we reach New York.

Then slam! bang! roar! a torpedo hit. Ship trembles and reels. Dishes, pots, pans, kettles crash to the floor. Shouts from outside. I feel a clutching at my throat, my knees are weak. I dash up to my cabin, get into my rubber suit, run out. Most of the people on board have gathered on deck. They are quiet—but every nerve is taut. The ship, not seriously damaged, keeps going full speed. We expect another torpedo, move about, go to look at the hole in the ship's side, sit down in the passageway, wonder if we may have got away from the sub.

At 02:30 a double hit. Two torpedoes ram the port side

looking toward the bow. The ship lists perilously. This is a death blow. Lifeboats are lowered. The sea runs high again and the boat in which I am sitting slaps against the ship's side, bounces up and down. People ease themselves overboard on ropes. Three fall into the water. We manage to pull one of them up; others are lying somewhere nearby crying for help. But we can't see anything, are driven backward. We must avoid the ship, row like crazy to stay clear of the propeller and keep the boat from capsizing. Sweat streams from us. Our hands get numb from frost and exertion. The biting wind whips our faces.

We hear a roar and catch the glitter of the submarine's cannons. A gigantic bonfire lights the black night; two rockets pencil a sparkling streak in the sinister red heavens.

The next morning four lifeboats manage to get together, two of them so battered that their crews must be taken over into ours. Our rudder is smashed and the sea is rough—we have to sacrifice the water kegs. The two boats tear loose and drift away.

Then work begins. The helmsman takes over, makes a drag anchor, rigs up a mast from two oars with backstays and all the necessary rigging, repairs the rudder, organizes. We divide ourselves into three watches of five men each, each watch to stand for three hours. Nine men are sick or too weak to work. So the struggle begins. We steer toward Newfoundland in our rickety sailboat. The craft itself is good except for the rudder; the mast stands in the middle of the boat; the lateen sail flutters, and the weight center is up front of the mast—the sick lie there under the tarpaulin. The off-watch seek refuge here for a little warmth and shelter against the storm and biting wind.

The days pass. The one like the other. Three meals. Our daily ration three ship biscuits spread with some kind of canned meat and half a glass of water. One night a rain; we open our mouths wide to catch some of it and get a few mouthfuls. One day we see birds. The fellow from Christiansand insists they are land birds . . . surely we must be close to land. Yes, one evening we think we see mountains in the distance. This is the fifth day. We are full of hope, in good spirits. But it isn't land after all.

The engineer isn't making it. He is already in a state of shock, restless and delirious, wants up and out. We restrain him by force. One night he dies. We remove his woolen sweater and bury him in the sea.

The mood on board is calm. If anyone begins to complain, he is either talked out of it or told to shut up. On the whole we are in good spirits. Often it does, to be sure, look bad and many a time the waves threaten to wash us overboard; but the helmsman spits at them, and that helps. We talk about other boats, other people, about what we shall have to drink when we have landed. One will have a glass of milk, one some tea, one prefers coffee. None will have liquor. Food is not so important. Now and then someone makes a witty remark, which brings a laugh. As, for instance, when "Christiansand" bursts out, "This is the third time I've been torpedoed. Now I'm beginning to get tired of it." And it wasn't meant as a joke.

One day, the sea being a little more calm, we sit talking about our lifeboat, saying nice things about it. We think it a fine one—no question about it. Really, after we have had a little rest we ought to fill it with gasoline and run it down to Halifax. That would be a fine trip. Ordinarily, however, our talk is "haul in here, ease up there, steer into the wind, change course, send up a rocket, light a flare." One thing is certain—everyone proposes to reach land. Those who are able do their utmost. No one takes advantage. All is share and share alike. The cigarette goes round from mouth to mouth. No one takes two puffs. Later a pipe stuffed with scraps of leftover tobacco and pocket muss makes the same round. The one helps the

other, massages the feet, hands his neighbor the water jug
no matter how tempting it is to take a swallow.

A dreadful storm rages, the worst so far. I have the feeling
of sitting in the air looking at myself and the others . . . con-
cluding that we must be queer to slave this way. I count the
intervals between the whitecaps—ten, twelve, fourteen seconds. Again and again we are about to capsize. Sea spray
froths in over the boat. Two are needed to bail out the water,
for it's more than just the torpedo hole in the side now. When
the situation is at its worst, the pumper stands at the rudder,
his face turned back to the waves. Breakers move threateningly toward us, foamy crest foremost. The hand of Death is
reaching out after us. The pumper eludes him. But he can't
hold on much longer; his hands are stiff and numb, full of
blisters and open sores. Yet he stands at his post till he is
relieved.

The spray freezes. In the course of the night it encrusts
the boat in an inch-thick shell of ice. The sail has to be requisitioned for an extension to the tarpaulin. We lie down under
it to rest, and fall asleep. Along in the night something stirs
at me—I don't know what. I come half awake, feel weak,
tired, and almost warm. I want to go back to sleep. Then it
dawns on me, "Now you are about to freeze to death." *This*
I will not do, and with what strength I have I raise myself
up, push off the ice-heavy canvas weighing me down like a
coffin lid where I lie in the passageway between the motor
compartment and the side bench. On top of the motor compartment lies "Aalesund" on his way to the eternal. We scuffle
to get a little warmth, then remember Duffy lying on the other
side of the compartment and try to rouse him.

But he has already crossed the bar. Four of us manage
to get him up . . . his arms and legs are rigid. We lay him
across a bench, massage him, warm him as much as we can.
Finally the second mate lies down on him and breathes into

his mouth. But Duffy has sailed his last voyage.

That morning we all talk less, are more quiet, and for the first time the thought of death comes to me. There is no terror in it. During the night I had experienced that there is no pain in freezing to death. But how ridiculous, how bitter, to be about to die. To leave forever those at home, and friends elsewhere . . . never more to participate with others. Then!—wouldn't you know it—there is that mate again. He laughs at me when I ask if we haven't gone east of Cape Race, and merely says, "No, we are, to be sure, headed in the right direction." That does it and up go the spirits. Presently we are once more sailing toward the coast.

All at once an airplane appears, an American one returning from convoy duty. We behave like insane, brandish oars, wave clothing, shout, whistle. The plane dives down over us. It has seen us—it has seen us! Later a destroyer comes, a Canadian one. Warm cabins, a tremendous lot of good food, hot coffee and bouillon, cigarettes—so much that it makes us dizzy. Now the skipper dies. He kept up all along in spite of being in a state of shock. He was determined to live, wanted to see the boat brought into harbor. That was the stimulus which kept his circulation functioning. When rescue came, when he no longer had to *will,* he collapsed and died. That was the ninth day.

The rest of us are alive, came to port the following day. It feels so miraculously safe to have land under foot again.

13

Shipwrecks and Rescues

"HELLO! THIS IS HENRIK..."

"Hello! This is Henrik speaking from New York. I come from southern Norway, am twenty-five years old, and left Norway last September to join the Navy. We had a hard trip across the North Sea—a three-day storm forced us to use the drog. Later, when we had fair weather, we developed motor trouble, so we hoisted sail. We then made right into port in England, though the trip took ten days. Our boat was very small, with only a five-mile motor, since it's difficult to get out of southern Norway with a large boat now that the coast is so heavily guarded. We did see a U-boat in the distance once but never learned whether she was German or English. It certainly gave us some tense moments. Later I was in the service of the Navy in Canada and got my training as a gunner—as a cannoneer, that is—for service in the Norwegian merchant marine.

"I signed on a ship on Christmas Eve and have since been sailing to England. My ship has crossed the Atlantic many times and there is probably no other ship that has carried so much fuel oil to England as this one has. On March 5 we were somewhere in the Caribbean Sea, sailing without a convoy. At 8:30 in the morning we were torpedoed. It caught us unawares—we had neither seen nor heard anything. We continued toward land at full speed, but an hour later we got a second hit. This time all hands took to the lifeboats. One man, a Frenchman, disappeared and we never saw him again; another was badly wounded; and several received minor injuries. One man was up at the top of the mast when the torpedo struck and he got a good shaking up, but he managed to survive.

"We had two lifeboats. One of them headed straight for land with most of the crew in it, including all the injured. The rest of us waited in the hope of boarding our ship again after dark, since she was still afloat, and then of getting her into port.

"So at night we went aboard, that is, the captain, the chief engineer, the bosun, the wireless operator, an AB seaman, a motorman, and the gunner, of course. We had been there about ten minutes, when cannons opened fire on us from both sides. Still we had seen nothing of the U-boat. The second or third shot hit our cannon and it exploded with an ear-splitting roar. All the men except one were injured, I got a terrific blow on the nose and a shell splinter in my left eye. It bled considerably and I could not see. I stood holding onto the ladder. Then the others called out that they were going into the lifeboat again. One man was seriously wounded and they lowered him into the lifeboat. I was the last man on the ladder. The others shouted to me to jump overboard, which I did, blindly. Once in the water, I could see again, since the salt water cleaned the one eye, and I swam over to the lifeboat. We rowed away with all our might and just in the nick of time, since the ship was now aflame. Half a minute more and we would not have managed to get away. As it was, every one of us was burned.

"We made toward shore. Our boat had a motor and the next morning we caught up with the other lifeboat and took it in tow. After forty-two hours we came to Abaco Island in the Bahamas, a Negro island with only three white families. We were quartered in a chapel and given first aid and bandages by a Negro nurse. The next day a hospital ship came over from Nassau and picked us up. One man had to remain on Abaco, however, since he was too sick to be moved. He died the following day. His name was Olaus Johansen and he had been a miner in Svalbard. After the raid on Svalbard he had gone to England. He was a stalwart man in his sixties. He was given doctor's care but unfortunately to no avail.

"Then we came to Nassau and were received at the pier by the Duke and Duchess of Windsor. I hardly caught a glimpse of them, however, since I was taken to the hospital immediately, but I heard they had been very kind. We were very well treated in every way, the sick and the well alike. All of us were given complete outfits by the Red Cross, though we heard that they came as a gift from the Duke.

"The others left after a week, but I remained in the hospital, because they had to remove my bad eye. Almost all the nurses were Negroes and it was a Negro doctor who removed my eye. Since all went well, I could leave a fortnight later. In Miami the official who heads the port authorities is a Norwegian, and there I was taken on a sightseeing tour of the town for a whole afternoon. Now I am waiting here to get a glass eye and then the Navy will have to decide what it wants to do with me."

A radio talk given in New York in April, 1942, by a young gunner from Svalbard.

What it does not tell is that this young gunner went to the Norwegian Medical Office in New York City and said: "Don't you dare put me out of active service; one eye is absolutely all you need for taking sight through a cannon."

TORPEDOED

BY CAPTAIN K. JOHNSEN

The S.S. *Ila* was on her way from Boston, U.S.A., to the United Kingdom with a cargo of steel and assorted goods. On October 5 about twelve o'clock the ship reached Sydney, Cape Breton [Nova Scotia], in convoy. We followed a varying course under orders from the commodore. The weather was changeful and at times stormy. On October 15 at about 4:45 the second ship ahead of the *Ila* sank. The crew was called and ordered to stand by at the lifeboats.

We steered clear of people and floating wreckage, and resumed the general course of the convoy. It was about 4:50. Shortly afterwards, at 4:55, our ship was hit by two torpedoes, one under hatch number 2 and one under the east side of the bridge. Violent explosions followed. The ship split in two and sank in about half a minute. Those of the crew who were standing by at the lifeboats were injured, presumably when loads of cargo and other things fell over them after the explosion. It was not possible to lower any of the boats. The one on hatch number 3 was smashed. The one on the boat deck was jammed under a davit when the stern plunged vertically into the deep.

The first mate, the first engineer, and two of the crew managed to get on top of the capsized motor lifeboat, but in spite of repeated attempts they could not right it. Later, First Engineer Hagbart Andersen died of wounds and exposure. The skipper and some of the crew were clinging to pieces of wreckage.

At about eight o'clock eight of the crew and the skipper were picked up by the French corvette *Mimosa*, Captain Boger Birot. The third engineer, Richard Andersen, and AB seaman George Falch, however, died within six hours, in spite of the persistent efforts of the crew on the corvette to save them by artificial respiration. The survivors were the skipper and seven men. They were put ashore at Reykjavik by the F.F.S. *Mimosa* on October 20.

NORWEGIAN SAILORS AS RESCUERS

Just as ships of other nations helped Norwegian sailors ashore after torpedoings, so Norwegians in countless instances saved shipwrecked crews of other countries. Letters tell their grateful stories. The first of those given below was published by the London *Nordisk Tidend*. The second appeared in the *Christian Science Monitor*, August 8, 1941.

I

M.S. *Heina*
Halifax, June 13, 1941

Captain A. Aardahl, M.S. *Heina*

DEAR SIR:

We the undersigned wish to thank you and your officers and men for the kindness, consideration and great hospitality which we have received at your hands during our stay aboard your noble vessel.

It was indeed a kindly fate that directed you to cross our path and rescue us from what might have been terrible suffering, privation, and finally death.

Only those who have experienced such an ordeal of four days and nights in an open boat at sea can realize and understand the heartfelt thanks and gratitude with which one is filled, and words seem inadequate to express.

We therefore wish you, Sir, and all your crew safe conduct in your travels and God grant that the struggle we are participating in as Allies, ends in success and restoration of your country back to pre-war, free and happier days.

Again thanking you from the bottom of our hearts, we remain, Sir,

Yours very respectfully,
Members of the crew of the
M.S. *Wellefield*

B. C. BENNETT, J. L. BROWNE, F. C. SMITH, G. W. CRUIK-SHANK, J. A. TAYLOR, E. R. TOMLINSON, J. SHARPLES, F. CARD, LEONARD HEYWOOD, JEFFREY CHEQUER, OLE ROVIK, F. NICHOLSON, J. KENNEY, C. H. JONES, JOHN REID

II

When the Dutch freighter *Maasdam* was torpedoed 400 miles off the coast of Greenland, among those who took to the lifeboats was Miss Lillian Evans of Arlington, Massachusetts, member of the Harvard Unit, numbering seventeen. Miss Evans was in the last lifeboat to leave the ship. This boat sank and she swam for hours before being picked up. Following are excerpts from letters to her mother, Mrs. Herbert T. Evans.

Aboard a Norwegian Tanker

I am safe and well, but have only the clothes on my back plus a sailor's pants and middy. All my things except your watch, Dick's medal, my class ring, and valuable papers and money are in Davy Jones's locker. Please don't worry, the Red Cross will take care of us. I am so glad I don't need all of life's luxuries.

We were on a Dutch ship which was sailing for England. June 27, at 1:15 A.M., the ship was torpedoed. We were all saved. Nine of the seventeen nurses are on the Norwegian tanker. We are just off the Hebrides, so in two days we will be in Barry Docks, Wales. We were going to Liverpool on the Dutch ship, but this one is going to Wales.

I am having wonderful new friendships; the Dutch are the very nicest people, and the Norwegians are perfect as sailors and as hosts to so many survivors.

I never wept a tear or felt any regrets, because I know everything will turn out right. My only thought when in the lifeboat was of you and in my mind was "Lead, Kindly Light" which I say every night when we have our "blackout." We were forty-nine ships in the convoy; forty-two are left.

I should like to tell you the details of our experience if I felt you wouldn't worry. Our lifeboat capsized and I swam in the water for hours until the Norwegians came out in their boat and took us in. They looked like Norse gods coming to me. They had on black rubber suits and yellow rubber hoods.

We still sleep fully dressed with our life jackets for pillows. . . . Of course this ship is very new, but is not for passengers, and so the captain gave us his suite—bedroom, living room, guest room, and bath—and nine girls managed well. We have a radio and phonograph with the best records.

The last two days no ships have been lost, and we are in too shallow water for submarines—so we have been washing and ironing the men's shirts and our own things.

Isn't it fortunate we didn't buy expensive shoes, shirts, etc., or any good street clothes? . . . You can't believe how cold we have been; wear sweaters and that heavy topcoat and fur-lined gloves all the time.

14

From Prison Ship to Prison Ship

David Faye Knudsen started out to be an engineer and studied for some years at the technical school in Trondheim but never finished his studies. In 1926 he yielded to a desire to go to sea, got his mate's certificate in 1931 and his master's certificate in 1934. During the first eighteen months of the war he crossed the Atlantic many times "scarcely aware of the war." Nothing happened—there had been a few air attacks, but that was all.

On March 5, 1942, he shipped with the old, slow 9,000-ton freighter *Aust,* captained by Christoffer Tuften, which left New York with a heavy cargo of cars and trucks. After a stop at St. Thomas in the Virgin Islands, March 15, they proceeded to Pernambuco, Brazil, for water and coal. Everyone felt perfectly safe, since these waters were not considered a danger zone.

On Good Friday, April 3, First Mate Knudsen was to stand watch from 4:00 to 8:00 P.M. Meantime he was resting on the couch in his cabin. Usually he rested in bed, but that day for some reason he chose the couch. At one o'clock there was a terrific roar and a violent crash. A shower of mirror glass flew through the cabin. He was thrown down, got up, rushed to the bridge. What was happening? The second mate was on duty. The skipper came up. No one had really *seen* anything. An attacking plane with motors stopped had slid down from the sun, and had started its motor and its machine gun at the same time, whence the deafening crash. It came back to drop two bombs. Both fell into the water, one close to hatch number 1, which it probably damaged.

The day was clear and fine. A ship was sighted about eight miles away and 30 degrees to starboard. Orders rang out: "Hard to port. Send SOS and inform what has happened." But there were no antennas! The airplane had been equipped with an apparatus which cut off the main antenna, the emergency antenna, and the cord between the bridge and the funnel for the steam whistle. It was impossible to establish contact with the world. "Clear at the gun." The raider opened fire. The Norwegian gun had too short a range; its shells hit the water far short of their target. Missiles from the raider whizzed round their heads, struck the ship, fell into the water on both sides of her. Some lifeboats were destroyed, riddled with holes. The captain gave orders to stop the engine and get into the lifeboats.

The lifeboats were lowered. One of them sank immediately, but all the men were picked up by the other boats. They were about twelve hundred miles off the coast [of Brazil], but in the pleasantly warm latitude of 20 degrees south they expected to be favored by the southeast trade wind which sweeps over the waves constantly in these seas. The boats would keep together and be tied to each other at night in order not to lose sight of one another. The men had agreed on all the details, only to learn to their great dismay that the raider had other plans for them. She approached the lifeboats, towering over them, and ordered all men to come on board. They climbed the ship's side as prisoners and saw their lifeboats destroyed by a wood-burning acid. The raider steamed over to the still-floating *Aust,* placed a bomb in her, waited until she sank, at about six o'clock in the evening, and steamed away immediately.

Seen at a distance the raider looked like a medium-sized fruit boat, but on board there were differences to be observed. Its crew of about 350 were dressed in khaki and shorts and navy caps. No cannons were to be seen on deck, only a few machine guns. But there were some very suspicious-looking large boxes suggesting crates for *cars.* The watchmen carried tommy guns.

The crew of the *Aust* was checked; every man had to give his name along with other information. The Germans were taken aback to find that the entire crew of forty was there and that not a single one showed as much as a scratch after the gunning. The captured men were made to take a salt-water bath and were given a very cursory examination by a German doctor. They were then sent below deck to a small room, perhaps eighteen feet by twenty-five, below the water line. It had no window but did have ventilation of a kind. Each man was issued a hammock, a cup, a tin bowl, a knife, fork, and spoon, a toothbrush, and some salt-water soap. There was very little room for the hammocks; they had to be taken down by day. The door to the adjoining room was open. It was already occupied by prisoners from two British ships seized two days earlier. One of them had been at St. Thomas when the *Aust* was there.

On the first day the Norwegians got no food because, said the Germans, "You had your meal aboard your ship"— which was true: they had been attacked just after noon. The next morning they began a kind of regular existence. The breakfast menu consisted of a not-bad dark bread, marmalade or artificial honey, and ersatz coffee; dinner of soup, also potatoes with lentils (peas or beans), and occasionally a small piece of meat; supper of bread, lard, and ersatz tea. At times there would be one can of sardines to each five or six men.

The "cabin" was so small there was hardly room to move around in it. The air was bad. There was nothing but artificial light all day, and from eight at night to eight in the morning there was no light at all. The men slept in the hammocks and used life belts for pillows. On the aft deck there was a toilet room with salt-water shower baths, and each man was given a washbasin. According to the schedule, the prisoners were to be allowed a forty-five-minute promenade on deck every day, but it was often omitted. The doctor made the rounds daily, as did the "prison officer," who asked them if there was anything they wanted. What many actually needed was clothing, since they had not been able to bring much of anything with them, but this was something they never got. The Germans confiscated all valuables and all money—most correctly of course, against a receipt to be validated in money at the nearest German consulate!

There was little to do all day long and the men had to find some way of occupying the time. They braided slippers from small pieces of string; played cards with cards of their own making; read old German magazines available in abundance and filled with propaganda from all fronts; took turns walking up and down the floor, since there was room for only a limited number at a time. Before long the officers were transferred to the same room as the British officers.

One day about a week after the capture of the *Aust* the Germans announced: "Tonight you'll have company." And they were right: late in the afternoon the raider captured another ship. It was an ugly affair. The German boat bore down on the ship and from a very close range used six-inch cannons, killing seventeen Britishers. For scouting the Germans used an Arados seaplane, which they kept somewhere below deck.

More than anything else the prisoners talked and thought about their future. What would happen to them? The stories they had heard were pretty much alike. Many Norwegians were known to have been sent home from France. But day by day the weather was getting warmer and everyone knew that the ship was rounding the Cape of Good Hope. When it became clear that the raider was in the Indian Ocean, everybody felt pretty low. No one had really foreseen Japan yet.

One day the Germans announced: "Prepare to leave." There wasn't much to prepare, but tension increased and all kinds of rumors filled the air. In the middle of the night, after a long period of waiting, the prisoners were transferred to large rubber rafts, as many as thirty to a raft, and towed by motorboats to the real prison ship. They had to climb up the side of the ship on a ladder. Here they found several minor differences. This ship, the *Regensburg,* was dirty and unpleasant, not as clean as the raider. There was less fresh water and it was almost impossible to keep clean. But there was one big advantage: since the ship was empty, the prisoners were allowed to remain on deck all day and did not have to stay in the hatch.

The raider went on but returned in a week with a rich prey; it had captured the British passenger liner *Nanking* with at least four hundred persons, including a large colored crew. Of British and Chinese there were twenty-seven women and children; they were placed together in hatch number 2. The day after the capture a baby was born on board the raider, but all went well. The British ship had been on her way from Australia to India with a cargo of food; the result was an agreeable change in the food situation everywhere on the *Regensburg.* Butter appeared for the first time in a long while. The women and children were allowed on deck with the men for two hours a day, and everyone tried to make the time as pleasant as possible. The Norwegians made swings for the children and joined in their play. After a few days the women and children, the wounded, and a number of British prisoners were transferred to a third German ship.

At times the Norwegians became very despondent when they saw how well organized the Germans were, how easily their ships managed to connect with each other. The entire communication system appeared to be directed from Berlin through some kind of secret short wave.

As the only prisoner who knew any German, David Knudsen was called upon to serve as interpreter in all kinds of situations and was consequently kept very busy. The prison officer told him that he had been on the *Altmark* in the Jössing Fjord in Norway! Two of the Germans had been on board the *Blücher* the night of April 9, 1940, when she was sunk in the Oslo Fjord with an enormous loss of men. The Germans were convinced the Norwegians had been prepared for the attack. "Oh, no; in that case you'd have got a very different reception," the Norwegians assured them.

The British officers knew the position at which their ship had been captured—about 25 degrees south and 80 degrees east, which made it possible for them to orient themselves somewhat.

Time passed more quickly now. A missionary gave Bible lessons. Someone made footballs and the crews played football on deck. Knudsen had two pupils who wanted to learn Norwegian; one was a British major in the medical service who had escaped from Singapore after its fall. Toilet paper had to do service for the improvised Norwegian grammar book. Since lack of proper clothing approached the catastrophe stage, some ambitious persons began making garments out of old flour sacks, using twist for stitching. The second mate was particularly skillful as a tailor; his trousers, when finished, proudly boasted BEST QUALITY in capital letters across the buttocks. Another boy ran about as a living advertisement for Shanghai Flour Mill.

The health situation was not good; there were many people of other races—Indians, Chinese, Negroes—and many of them developed scabies from lack of water and soap.

The ship sailed through Sunday Strait between Java and Sumatra. Land was visible on both sides. But probably no one contemplated escaping. No one wanted to fall into the hands of the Japs—and there would have to be at least *some* chance of success even in the most desperate attempt.

On July 12 the ship arrived at Yokohama. The white people and the dark-skinned were separated; the Norwegians were sent to the German ship *Ramses,* which lay in the harbor. They lived in the hatch, got better food and as much fresh water as they wanted, but no clothing. After a month the British prisoners were put ashore and sent to a prison camp, but since Japan was not at war with Norway, the Japs disclaimed any responsibility for or interest in the Norwegian prisoners. There were wild rumors; someone said that there were more than one hundred Norwegian prisoners on different ships in the harbor and that they would be sent back to Europe on German ships trying to break the blockade. It was dull in Yokohama. News did of course come through, but it was strongly colored by the German radio-press and the Japanese newspapers in English. You may be sure it was bad news, though the truth did at times make its own way through the web of censorship, lies, and propaganda. The Norwegians were therefore very skeptical when the Germans continued advancing in the streets of Stalingrad for three months!

The Norwegians were held in the port of Yokohama for three months, part of the time on the British ship *Nanking.* To pass the time they volunteered to work, which among other things consisted in sorting provisions and gave rich opportunity for stealing all kinds of food and tobacco. The pay was an extra five cigarettes a day, added to the ordinary ration of three. The clothing problem grew steadily worse since absolutely nothing was ever given out. Soles for wooden slippers were cut with table knives, canvas was used for straps. A Lithuanian sailor particularly skilled in wood carving made an excellent chessboard and a set of chessmen.

From time to time crews from other torpedoed Norwegian ships arrived. There was, for example, the entire crew of the *Kattegatt*, which had been captured by another German raider. On August 20 sixteen of the *Aust*'s crew, together with the crews of two Norwegian tankers, the *Madrono* and the *Herborg*, were sent to Europe on the *Dresden*, and all reached Norway safely. As a rule there were six or seven German ships in the harbor; about once a month one of them would set out for Europe and try to break the Allied blockade. The Norwegians estimated that three German raiders were operating in the Atlantic at the time.

Some weeks later another part of the *Aust*'s crew was put aboard the *Regensburg* to be sent to Europe, but the ship was torpedoed in Sunday Strait by an American submarine. She did not, however, sink and managed to limp into Singapore for repairs. It is not known whether she ever proceeded from there.

On October 10 three men, the last contingent from the *Aust*, were put aboard the *Ramses* to be sent to Europe. With them were seven men from the *Kattegatt*. The *Ramses* loaded in Kobe and coaled in Balikpapan; from there it proceeded to Batavia in Java to take on a cargo of rubber.

In Yokohama the Norwegian prisoners had little contact with the natives, but David Knudsen and many of the others had had a good deal of opportunity to know the Far East well from their frequent earlier visits; and besides, in spite of their imprisonment, the men were always meeting old friends. In Kobe they met an old friend, a stevedore-foreman

with the un-Japanese name of *Olav!* His godfather was a
Norwegian captain, he declared, and he looked as if he
might have some European blood in his veins. Said Olav,
"Japan very tired damned war." Balikpapan in Sumatra had
fared badly; from the ship the prisoners had seen the demolished oil refinery with its tanks toppled over. Its landscape
was spotted with black traces of gigantic fires in once beautiful forests. In Batavia it was not possible to get into the harbor;
the Dutch had sunk four big vessels between the moles and
completely closed the entrance; the loading had to take place
from small lighters and required ten or eleven days instead of
the usual two or three. Japanese magazines showed beautiful
pictures of Japanese children waving Japanese flags and enthusiastically greeting the "liberator." The Norwegian prisoners had seen these. But the longshoremen had quite another
story to tell: "No beer, no cigarettes, no clothing; Nippon
man take everything." And they asked how long it would be
before the Americans arrived.

The Norwegians on the German ship hoped and prayed
for one thing: help from the Allies. A couple of Danes on
board were, however, more cautious and warned the Norwegians against expressing themselves so freely to the Germans, who had the power to take revenge. And the Norwegians laughed. "We'll say what we like. The British will
soon be here!" And that same day they *did* come!

Captain Tuften and his first mate, David Knudsen, were
having an afternoon nap, when the siren began screaming.
The second mate rushed in to announce a ship. "We were
frantic with joy. Through the scuttles we could look out and
watch the signals." The *Ramses* had hoisted the Norwegian
flag, and for a terrible moment it looked as if she was able
to bluff her pursuers, for the British ship changed her course
and appeared to be moving off. But then orders followed:
"Stop the engines! Everybody into the boats!" The Germans

were quiet and disciplined, and behaved well. They sank their own ship with a delayed-action mine which exploded after eight minutes. Bullets sprayed the doomed ship from every direction, from an Australian and from a Dutch cruiser; the projectiles whizzed through the air around the lifeboats and enormous columns of water shot into the air.

The *Ramses* had good anti-aircraft defenses but only one cannon and it was made of wood! Just a piece of wood in order to make the ship look like a freighter belonging to one of the Allies. The wooden cannon drifted about in the sea while the *Ramses* was sinking and was enthusiastically photographed by the crews of the victorious ships. In the cargo of the *Ramses* were several pigs, and one of them actually was saved from the wreck and triumphantly brought aboard the Australian cruiser. Here it received a special decoration: a red ribbon with the inscription "War Prisoner No. 1." Norwegians and Germans were huddled together in the same lifeboat. Most of the men sat silent and depressed. The Norwegians jumped up and down, laughing and singing and waving until the Australians didn't know what to make of it. No human life was lost in this happy capture—only a few pigs. The Germans thought themselves lucky to be taken aboard the Australian instead of the Dutch cruiser. "The Dutch hate us so terribly," said one of them. "No wonder," said another.

From then on David Knudsen's story is filled with joy and happiness. The treatment aboard the Australian cruiser was wonderful; the men got decent food and good clothing. When they had left Japan, every man received a polo shirt and an overall; now they were given officer's uniforms. And there was the voyage along the coast of Australia in the first-class cabins of the liner *Mauretania*. It is hard to find words to describe the pleasure which luxuries gave them again—a decent bathroom, a dining room with waiters. And the feeling of ground under their feet—the Norwegians had not set foot on land from March 16 to December 2, 1942, more than nine months. Then the ten Norwegians believed lost arrived at Sydney, where they could report at the office of the Norwegian Shipping and Trade Mission.

15

The Wreck of the S.S. "Blink"

I

BY BIRGER LUNDE

Sunday, February 8, 1942. Arrived at Charleston at 7 P.M.

Monday, February 9. Started filling bunkers at 8 A.M. Left Charleston at 6 P.M. with pilot on board. At 7:30 P.M. the pilot left the ship. We continued according to the route indicated.

Wednesday, February 11. Wind N, strength 5, sea N, strength 4. At 8:45 P.M. the S.S. *Blink* was hit aport by a torpedo which passed through hatch number 2 without exploding and went out starboard. About forty-five seconds later she was hit by two more torpedoes, both striking midship in the engine room. Two vigorous explosions followed. The ship started heeling to port and the captain ordered all men to the lifeboats. The captain and AB seaman O. Numme were on the bridge at the time of the torpedoing. Ordinary seaman O. Sahlin was at the helm. The third mate, who also functioned as a radiotelegrapher, was in the radio room; according to what he told later, the station was destroyed by the explosions so that no radio message could be sent out. The port lifeboat was smashed by the explosion, leaving only the starboard one for use. On board the *Blink* were one rubber safety suit and one life belt for every man. Twenty-three men got into the lifeboat.

The following were believed to have been killed by the explosions: Dahlman, first engineer; K. Johansen, donkeyman; Roos (Dutch), stoker; Sitrman, mess boy; Lewis (British), gunner. Two men were seen on deck after the starboard life-boat had been lowered; they were believed to be H. Gillik (South African), stoker, and A. Pappacena (British), galley boy. We shouted to them to jump overboard and said we would pick them up. They did not do it. They went aft and unfastened the raft, and probably succeeded in lowering it on the water, since we saw weak lights under the stern.

At 21:10 P.M. the *Blink* went down. We decided to stay at drag anchor all night, hoping to find the raft at daylight.

Thursday, February 12. All night we had a northeast breeze and a heavy sea. At daylight we were not able to find the raft. We now set sail and made for land. At 10:45 our lifeboat was caught by a heavy sea and capsized. It continued to float, bottom up. Everybody hung onto the keel, and we succeeded in righting the boat. In the capsizing seaman R. Graves was drowned. K. Johansen, third mate, tried to rescue him, but in vain. All the provisions, including bread and water, were torn loose and went overboard. After the boat had been righted, we swam about for a time while two men got into it and tried to bail out the water. Everyone came back on board. The boat floated on the tanks, but when all the men were in it, the water came about a half foot above the gunwale. At 11:00 A.M. it capsized again. We managed to get it back on an even keel. At 1:00 P.M. we capsized a third time. We got it back once more. We tried several times to bail out the water, but in vain. We sat in water up to our breasts.

At 5:00 P.M. ordinary seaman K. Larsen went insane and died.

At 6:30 P.M. ordinary seaman P. Winther went insane and died.

At 7:00 P.M. a ship passed about half a mile away. We did our best to signal her with a boathook and an oilskin, but she passed without seeing us. Half an hour later another ship passed, a bit closer. We signaled her in the same way, but without success.

At about 7:00 P.M. third mate K. Johansen went insane and died.

At about 9:00 P.M. cook Eriksen went insane and died.

At about 10:00 P.M. ordinary seaman F. George went insane and died.

At about 10:30 P.M. ordinary seaman O. Sahlin went insane and died.

Friday, February 13. Wind northerly, strength 6, sea from north, strength 4. We drifted before wind and current. Our lifeboat was about a half foot under water. The heavy sea washed over us constantly.

At about 1:00 A.M. coal heaver J. Donace went insane and died.

At about 3:00 A.M. Captain S. Ulvestad went insane and died.

At about 4:30 A.M. third engineer Sorensen went insane and died.

At about 5:00 A.M. second mate K. Johansen went insane and died.

At about 7:00 A.M. gunner J. White went insane and died.

All day passed without sighting anything. Wind and sea kept on being heavy and bailing was impossible in spite of several attempts.

Saturday, February 14. Wind northerly, strength 6, sea

from north, strength 4. We were drifting before wind and current. The lifeboat continued being under water. The sea inundated the boat all the time.

At about 4:30 A.M. stoker Kvia went insane and died.

At about 7:00 A.M. ordinary seaman E. Plume went insane and died.

At about 9:00 A.M. ordinary seaman A. Hennum went insane and died.

At about 11:00 A.M. stoker M. Larsen went insane and died.

At about noon second mate F. Feydt went insane and died.

At 3:30 P.M. we sighted a ship and signaled her as well as we could. She saw us, and after about twenty minutes we were taken aboard the S.S. *Monroe,* Captain W. W. Clendaniel. On board the *Monroe* we were well treated and given good nursing care.

The following were rescued: B. Lunde, first mate; H. Friis, steward; A. Numme, AB seaman; A. Torbjörnsen, AB seaman; G. Gulliksen, stoker; G. Johnstone, ordinary seaman.

Tuesday, February 17. At noon the *Monroe* arrived at Baltimore. Ordinary seaman G. Johnstone was taken to the hospital immediately. The others were taken to a Coast Guard station, where we were questioned as to what had happened. Afterwards we were all brought to the hospital.

SIGNED: O. NUMME, stoker
G. GULLIKSEN, stoker
B. LUNDE, first mate [the writer]

II

BY TOR MYKLEBOST

There had been twenty-three men in the lifeboat out on the open sea, and around them darkness and violent wind.

Six had come safely to shore after four days of drifting. The other seventeen had fought in vain against the elements. One after the other they had broken down and "remained in the sea," as they say in Norwegian, even though their comrades had tried desperately to save them.

I found four of the survivors in the Norwegian Seamen's Home in Baltimore. They were First Mate Birger Lunde, AB seamen Odd Numme and A. Torbjörnsen, and stoker Godtfred Gulliksen. Steward H. Friis and ordinary seaman G. Johnstone were still in the hospital.

"But there's nothing much wrong with them," said the first mate. "At least not with the steward. It's just a safety precaution on the part of the doctor. They sent all of us to the hospital; some kind of formality, no doubt."

He smiled shyly, almost as if he ought not say, "But it certainly felt good to sleep in a decent berth again!"

The others laughed happily. And Gulliksen added: "One evening in the lifeboat I thought I was in a nice, cozy room—pure imagination, of course. And there was a big, warm bed with clean sheets and a huge down comfortable." Gulliksen tried to sketch out the bed with his hands. "And so I went to bed, you see. In the middle of the Atlantic Ocean! I just kind of imagined things, you understand." He laughed uproariously. The others joined in.

I looked at the boys. They were rather young, none over thirty. There was the first mate, twenty-eight, his features clean and weather-beaten, his eyes clear and watchful. His skin might have been made of leather. He was still "First Mate" to his comrades, even here in the Seamen's Home where all ranks disappear, and was regarded as having authority by comrades who don't ask for stripes or stars.

Seaman Odd Numme was tall and blond, and had a slouchy walk. Every now and then he would toss his head energetically to fling back the unruly blond lock which was constantly slipping down on his forehead. His strong, brown working hands lay quietly on the table in front of him. Arthur Torbjörnsen looked like a boy. He had thoughtful blue eyes. He didn't say much. And there was the stoker, Godtfred Gulliksen, slight, blond, and bubbling over with high spirits—happy-go-lucky, the Yanks would say.

Those four boys had just gone through an experience which it is hard for any landlubber to imagine. And it seemed to have left no traces on them. Along with two other comrades, they were the only survivors of the worst Norwegian shipwreck in this war so far, but they didn't look deeply impressed. They had been rescued, had been lucky, as the first mate put it; and they wanted to go out again after their holiday of a month. Their chief concern seemed to be to find out whether they could rent a shack or a country cottage in Connecticut and do some skiing for a few weeks. They were certainly not eager to talk about their experiences. After a time I managed to persuade them to tell their story.

On the second day the tragedy had grown to big dimensions. A stiff wind came from the northeast. One after the other of the shipwrecked went insane and died. This began on Thursday evening and went on through Friday and Saturday afternoon until the lifeboat was rescued.

The four of them told about the events very simply, without any dramatizing. They told how they had tried in vain to save the lives of their comrades. The first mate said: "In such a case, where the cold is not too intense, I think the effect of the strain is as much psychological as physical. The ones who first lost courage and hope were the first to succumb. And it really did look almost hopeless, particularly at night." "Well," objected Gulliksen, "perhaps you are right, but I'm not sure. I had sworn that I'd reach shore, but it certainly is through no merit of mine that I'm sitting here today." He looked at Numme, who moved away, blushing like a schoolboy: "That boy fetched me out of the sea three times! My imagination was running wild, you see. Once I thought I was in the nice, warm room with that bed I told you about. Another time I wanted to take a taxi right behind the boat! I wanted to go to a hotel just up the hill. I saw it as plainly as I see you right now!" He was smiling. "I wasn't the only one to see it either! We all saw it at the same time."

The others agreed. At one time practically everyone had seen that taxi and the hotel. And one after the other had gone overboard to take it. "Why do we go on sitting here in this restaurant?" they would be asking. "Can't we ride up to the hotel?" Gulliksen went on: "It is damned queer. I remember it very clearly. And somehow I must have realized even then that it was just imagination. But I could not help it. I told myself that it was bunk, but all the same I really did see it: there the taxi was, and right up the hill the hotel! And I was very sleepy." And he remembered other thoughts. "I had to have an injection. The first mate and the others explained to me that I was just making up things, and I *did* think it awfully silly. But I felt I *must* take that injection, so I undressed."

The following things were told later and not in the presence of the first mate, Lunde, and AB seaman Numme; they didn't like to be praised. But it was Lunde and particularly Numme to whom the others owed their lives. Both of them fought like lions to keep up the spirits of their comrades and prevent them from losing hope. Time and again Numme plunged into the sea to fetch back a comrade who had jumped in, without noticing or caring about the sharks which crowded around the boat. His two comrades say of him: "He held us when we grew rebellious. He would go on joking with us and didn't give up until we had calmed down. He never gave in as long as there was a chance. He even thrashed us unmercifully to keep us warm. And he tried it with all of us. But don't tell him we told you, because he'll get furious if he finds out."

Another little side light was not without interest. The crew of the American ship, the S.S. *Monroe,* which rescued the survivors, spoke about Numme almost reverently. "Nobody could see that he had been in a lifeboat for four days," they said. "He actually looked as though he had just had a refreshing sleep."

They sat in front of me, the four of them in new suits. These were the only clothes they had; they had been half naked when they reached shore. They spoke quietly and thoughtfully, most about events in Norway: "How are things in Bergen, in Sandefjord, in Grimstad, at Nötteröy?" They wanted every detail I could give.

"It must be awful at home," they said. And they mentioned that one of their comrades who had gone down with the *Blink* had left Norway only four months ago. "His wife had just had a baby." They recalled that it was twelve days old when he left. "So you must know it is terrible at home, when he could do a thing like that." They kept silent for a while.

Sailors never say their comrades died. "He went west," they say. And Gulliksen all of a sudden grew serious: "I've learned this, that if I have to go west, I want to be drowned. It is not a painful death." He seemed to be listening to his own words, and the usual smile came creeping back: *"If I have to go west! Godtfred Gulliksen is immortal."* They all laughed again, happily and boyishly. The eyes in those brown weather-beaten faces were strong and vivacious.

As I left, they said: "See you in Norway. It won't be long now."

16

Forty-eight Days on a Raft

In 1939, Olaf Brekke shipped on the 12,000-ton M.S. *Moldanger,* a beautiful modern refrigerated ship carrying assorted cargo, and he stayed with this vessel until she was sunk. The captain was Björn Hansen, whose brother, president of the Norwegian Shipowners Association, is now a prisoner in Germany. "A fine skipper and a swell guy" is what carpenter Brekke thinks of his skipper.

They had been in the Atlantic not far from the coast of the United States when the *Moldanger* was hit by her first torpedo. The missile struck the engine and blew up the air compressor and the ammonia supply for the refrigerators. Two men on watch in the engine room were killed instantly; the radio was put out of commission and one lifeboat was dashed to the deck and demolished. In three minutes the water stood over the top of the engine and the ship went right down. The motorboat was put off. It filled with water from the deck, but they managed to get away from the side of the ship in time. The starboard lifeboat was stuck and could not be freed. The port lifeboat was just being lowered, when a second torpedo hit right under it, killing twelve men. "It was plain murder; that torpedo was completely unnecessary," says Brekke with bitterness in his voice; "the ship was sinking anyway." Brekke himself was wounded and lost consciousness for a moment in the second explosion. He had then been aft helping the skipper and the chief engineer put a raft on the water. The three were the last to leave the ship. The water had reached deck level, and they swam over to the raft.

At daylight the men on the raft found the motorboat, which had been cruising around hoping to pick up some more survivors. A lot of wool from the cargo came floating to the surface and two bodies drifted past. The U-boat came to the motorboat and asked for the captain; at that time the subs had the unpleasant habit of taking the captains of torpedoed ships prisoner and bringing them to Germany. But they got the reply that so far as was known the skipper had gone down with the ship, which was what the people in the motorboat seriously feared.

The motorboat was full of water and they had to keep bailing it out all the time; and it had several badly wounded men on board. The gig was all right in spite of some damage. For three or four days the three boats kept together; then the weather worsened, and it was evident that medical attention was urgently needed for the wounded men. They agreed that first the gig and then the motorboat were to head for land and get assistance for the others. The third mate had the gig; the captain the motorboat. And for the men on the raft the real odyssey began.

It would be difficult to imagine one of those contraptions —a crate nine by eleven in size, with barrels for floaters, a frame and a kind of railing around it, and a protecting canvas for a top. There is scarcely any room for movement on such a raft, especially on one where five men have to be together. Here two rafts were fastened together.

Most of the men carried both a life belt and a rubber safety suit, and seaboots; the safety suits proved to be warm and very practical. But the other men, not thus provided, also managed well; they had their usual work clothes plus oilskins of the kind used by fishermen in Norway. Moreover, the rafts were amply equipped with sweaters, lumberjackets, and the like. No one complained of the cold except during the three cyclones. It was the warm season of the year and that accounts for a good deal.

The fare was simple: water and bread. Nearly all of the bread had been spoiled by salt water, but fortunately the drinking water was all right. One small cup of water per person per day was the ration. Then there were a few milk tablets and vitamin tablets; at first every man got five a day, later four or three.

This is the crew list. Their ages range from nineteen to fifty-nine.

> Olaf Brekke, carpenter
> Kaare Kaarstad, electrician
> Einar Moldekliev, machinist
> John Bakkemyr, AB seaman
> Johan Hansen, AB seaman
> Harald Revaa, ordinary seaman
> David Holgersen, steward
> Paul W. Andersen, messboy (Danish)
> Holger Aronson, messboy (Swedish)

Life on board was quickly organized. A regular four-hour watch was established on each raft, just as on an ordinary ship. Using oars for masts, they tried to sail toward the coast of the United States, but wind and current were against them. The rations lasted twenty-one days, and everybody was pretty depressed the day the supply gave out. Fortunately a cyclone arrived at the right moment, pouring considerable rain water into the sail, and they could fill the water tank again; that helped revive morale. Along about the same time the boys started fishing. The rafts were now drifting with the Gulf Stream, which carried them far away from the United States, and with it came long strands of yellow Saragossa seaweed which seemed to lure the fish. The men had to improvise some kind of fishing tackle; a two-foot piece of wire served for a line and a safety pin for a hook. They could not of course catch very big fish, nothing larger than six or seven inches; but they got enough to allow each man a fish or two a day. And the taste was excellent, not a bit salty. They removed the entrails except for the liver, which they ate conscientiously, thinking of vitamins. Catfish in particular had a fine liver but were very hard to catch with primitive apparatus. The menu as a rule was limited to dolphin, which seemed to be biting eagerly enough.

And the days passed well enough. There were all kinds of things to do. Someone was always fishing and two men kept watch constantly. One man was at the helm. Several times they tried sailing. Everyone was soaked most of the time, but a couple of times the sun came out and then the clothes were put out to dry; that was very nice. Or they would take a swim in the great Atlantic, for it was fine to get a little exercise now and then. One man had to be on the lookout for sharks, which were numerous. Sharks were a godsend, though—they brought with them that most delectable tidbit of the whole trip and the urgently needed change in the monotonous diet, namely the nice, big yellow and brown turtle! The turtles tried to get away from the sharks and were evidently looking for a safer haven, "and we were looking for them." The boys managed to catch three of them—one man got hold of the flippers and another helped him haul the victim on board. They were huge beasts, "beautiful to look at but even better to eat." They must have weighed fifty or sixty pounds. In order to handle them properly the men tethered them until daylight. The meat was firm and good; the blood had a fine flavor and was no doubt mainly responsible for the excellent physical condition which the men managed to maintain during this ordeal of seven weeks. One entirely unexpected com-

plication arose, however: one of the men, being a vegetarian,
declared that he could not deviate from his principles! Finally,
after a long struggle with his conscience and with starvation
imminent he accepted some of the meat but energetically
refused to drink the blood.

After twenty-eight days they sighted a ship and sent up a
blue flare. But perhaps because it was early and the morning
somewhat foggy, the ship did not see them; at least she gave
no sign of doing so. After thirty-six days a Liberty ship appeared. She was making directly for the rafts and was hardly
a mile away; everybody was delighted and the men wanted to
drink the rest of the water to celebrate. But Brekke would not
allow it. "We are not there yet," he said, with a kind of
premonition that they were not going to be taken aboard.
He had the feeling of having lived through it once before, in
a dream perhaps. And he was right: the ship turned away—
probably suspecting that the rafts with their red sails were
nothing but a submarine trap.

That was an awful blow. "Were we mad at those idiots!"
On the other hand, no one seemed ever to have any serious
doubt about their future; all felt sure they would be picked
up some day. The only question was when.

Usually spirits were good. The men sang, talked about
matters in general, or discussed the war situation. And of
course there were endless discussions about food, about what
each preferred, what they were going to have for their first
meal on shore. No one slept any too well, and indigestion
caused considerable trouble; in fact, everyone suffered from
it. After forty-five days they drank a little sea water. This
always takes effect immediately; but it is dangerous to drink
too much. It rained three times, making it possible to keep up
the water rationing faithfully. Once the cyclone was so violent
that in spite of torrents of rain they were unable to collect
any water at all. Another time the mast broke down and they

rigged up an emergency mast—another oar. "We could hardly expect to row the Atlantic anyway."

Many details came to light during the conversation, things which had been almost forgotten during the six months which had passed. Thirst was the great problem. It was hard to swallow the fish and the tablets without drinking anything with them. Lips got chapped. One man was rather seriously wounded and had to undergo extended surgical treatment after his arrival in the United States. Everyone's appearance changed: "The barber shop was closed." Everyone lost weight, from forty to fifty-eight pounds each, as they realized later on.

On the forty-eighth day a Norwegian ship picked up the crew. Every man was able to climb the ship's side without help—nobody was too exhausted for that. And all agreed heartily that they could have managed a few more days— things were after all not so very bad. Legs were a bit wobbly and all complained of abrasions caused by constant dampness and lack of exercise. But what did that matter! Life and honor had been saved.

The reception aboard the rescuing ship was wonderful, of course. The crew almost fought to give away their clothes. And the first meal, which consisted of one slice of bread, some gruel, and a soft-boiled egg, tasted far better than any of the meals which they used to imagine in the lifeboat could possibly have tasted. As for the first bath—it just could not be described. And among themselves the crew fought to give their own berths to their shipwrecked compatriots, until they remembered the passenger accommodations, "which we got free of charge."

Back in New York! The skipper, Björn Hansen, had just received the good news the night before and was at the quay to welcome the long-lost men. Red Cross ambulances came down, but happily they were not needed. One could tell by the expression on the captain's face how happy he was. Though not a man given to a demonstration of his feelings, he did not leave the men for a second that first day. It was just three days before that he had reported the men "missing" and in all likelihood given up hope.

What has happened to the men since then? Most of them are out sailing again; but all agree that they have their carpenter, Olaf Brekke, to thank for the happy ending, for it was he who was responsible for the excellent discipline aboard. And there have been interviews and the war medal and other medals which Brekke mentions with a shy smile. He has been interviewed by Vera Zorina before an audience of three thousand in Brooklyn.

The last word goes to the Director of Shipping, Mr. Oivind Lorentzen, who sent Brekke a photograph of the raft crew with this inscription: "Thanks for a splendid deed, worthy of Norwegian seamen."

P.S. The publication *Reports From the Director of Shipping* of September 3, 1942, states that there were two doctors aboard the *Washington Express,* which rescued the men on the raft. In reporting their medical observations these doctors say among other things: "The story of how the shipwrecked men managed to get hold of food is an excellent example of what people who are used to relying on themselves are able to do in the face of the greatest difficulties. Perhaps the most typical illustration is the way they went about procuring fat. The turtles which were caught had a thick layer of fat beneath the carapax; the fat, however, was not palatable and was hard to swallow. They had therefore to set up a fat refinery on a small scale. The fat was collected, put in a box, and exposed to the sun in the middle of the day. In that way it was melted, and the muddy sediment settling to the bottom left the liquid above it clear, fine, and good-tasting—'almost like first-class butter,' said the men when they came ashore. They dried the fish they caught for thirty-six hours and then dipped them in the fat."

France

17

Dunkirk and Calais

BY JACOB WORM-MÜLLER

In the old charter parties the text read: "I, N.N., skipper next to God on the ship consigned to me." This is one of the secrets of our leading position at sea. The attitude explains why our skippers, without exception, instead of being misled by Quisling's telegrams on April 9, 1940, instantly put themselves at the service of their King and legal Government. It is this sense of responsibility which has made our skippers self-reliant and which enables them to act wisely and decisively in the most difficult and confused situations. I do not know of anything that could give a better demonstration of this than the unique exploits of Norwegian ships in May and June of 1940, when they saved thousands of soldiers and civilians from the onrushing German army. Dunkirk, Calais, and Brest will also be names honored in Norwegian history.

One of these heroes, Captain Fredhjem of the M.S. *Hird,* recently received the War Cross, the highest of distinctions. His is a brilliant example of what can be achieved by the genuine royal guard.

The *Hird* arrived at Dunkirk on May 8, 1940, with a cargo of coal. Unloading was exceedingly difficult, particularly after May 13, when the town was being bombed in-

cessantly. By May 17 the cargo had been discharged. In a
this confusion new instructions were, however, not to be had
for both the consul and the agent of the line had left th
town. The skipper therefore decided to sail in ballast. This th
French authorities refused to allow and ordered him instea
to take on a big load of wheat. The skipper protested on th
ground that it was unfeasible, since the ship had to chang
docks repeatedly because of the bombing and because prac
tically all of the lighters had by this time been sunk. Th
skipper then received orders to take on a cargo of wool, bu
before the bales could be loaded they were destroyed by in
cendiary bombs.

For two weeks the *Hird* was in the line of fire day and
night. Many of the bombs fell close to the ship, some on th
pier, others in the water a few yards away. The explosion
shook the whole ship, and the ship's side was full of hole
above the waterline. On May 26, an English munitions shi
close by blew up. It blasted all the doors and casings in th
Hird, and big pieces of iron from the exploded ship raine
down on the deck. On May 28 the situation grew so seriou
that the French Admiralty gave the captain orders to leave
with as many soldiers as his ship could take. At seven o'clock
in the evening the embarkation began; by ten o'clock it wa
finished. Fifteen hundred British and two thousand French
soldiers, besides civilian refugees, were crowded into the ship
The *Hird* had orders to follow a French ship with fourteen
hundred passengers aboard, but shortly after midnight tha
ship struck a mine and sank. Shortly after that a smaller
steamer hit a mine and disappeared. Next morning the *Hird*
met a British destroyer which had been hit by a torpedo but
was still afloat. In every single instance the *Hird* tried to save
the survivors in spite of the danger from German airplanes
Later she rescued the crew from a torpedo boat and other
boats and then started full speed ahead, arriving in Cherbourg

on May 30, where the troops were disembarked. From there she proceeded directly to Cardiff for repairs.

This was a brilliant seaman's exploit. But other ships also distinguished themselves. Seven Norwegian ships lay in Brest under the worst of bombings. One of them left with five or six hundred men aboard. Others were in Le Havre under similar conditions.

A Norwegian ship of 2,500 tons arrived in Calais on May 17 with a cargo of coke after having called at Boulogne. The town was already in panic over the droves of Belgian and French refugees which were pouring in. Aerial attacks added to the confusion of the population and the nervousness of the French authorities. Ships leaving the harbor often struck magnetic mines that had been dropped by German airplanes, and detonations constantly came in from the sea. The captain never lost his head. Since there were no responsible authorities left to make decisions, he had to act on his own. He, as well as the crew, went without sleep for many days. Conditions in the ship became unbearable. His own ship and another Norwegian ship lay in the direct line of fire. Bombs fell all around them. They tried to shoot down the planes, but the planes were too swift. When the ship had finished unloading and the captain asked for permission to leave port, his request was refused. Realizing that the town was surrounded, he decided to take matters in his own hands and get out of the trap. He managed to get the gates of the dock open, but found that no tugboat was to be had. The ship had to go out backwards through the two narrow mouths. Had it not been for the excellent cooperation between captain and engineer, the feat would have been impossible. When the ship came alongside a wharf to take on refugees, a terrible struggle began. Soldiers, men of all ages, and desperate mothers with babies tried to get aboard. Terrible scenes were enacted on the wharf, and the crew did everything to prevent those up in front from

being pushed into the water between the ship and the whar
Suddenly a German plane flew in. The people rushed up th
gangplank, which broke under them. Frantic cries and deafer
ing yells reverberated from everywhere, from sea, land, an
ship. Finally the decks were overcrowded; 1,125 persons ha
come on board, and among them about 450 children and 10
French soldiers. All the other ships had left Calais, and thi
was the last ship to go out.

But difficulties were not ended. The danger of mines wa
overwhelming. The skipper had no sailing route. He signale
a French lighthouse and asked for the right course, but go
some very strange answers. The Germans had already take
over the station! Having therefore to be a "skipper next t
God," he had to decide for himself what course to tak
through the mine-infested waters, and succeeded in reachin
Dover and later Southampton.

The voyage was a nightmare with terrified refugees wh
became panic-stricken from the air attacks and explodin
mines. Several became insane, and a French soldier jumpe
overboard. The weeping and whimpering of the children go
on everyone's nerves. But the skipper and his crew were equa
to their task. Overtired as they were after many sleeples
nights, they gave up their cabins to refugees. The captai
took care of the distribution of milk to the children. The stew
ard baked bread, and made water gruel, and tried to distribut
it as fairly as possible. "This was not easy to manage," say
the captain in his stirring report, "but I thought all the whil
of the words of the Bible about the five thousand persons wh
were fed out of two loaves of bread and five small fish. I ha
to try to do something like it."

It was a miracle that he managed to keep discipline amon
the passengers, which he could not have done had it not bee
for the quiet manner, cool-headedness, and profoundly huma
attitude of his crew. They alone made it possible. The cap

tain writes: "Many things may be said about Norwegian sailors. They can take a drink and cause their captain many worries. But I was mighty proud of the Norwegians in Calais. There was no sign of panic among them. Courageous and helpful, they tried to do their best in an awkward situation. I had to smile when I saw one of the stokers who had given me lots of trouble because I could not procure any money come rushing up the gangway with a little boy in one hand and a screaming baby girl on his arm. It was touching to see the big clumsy stoker trying to comfort the screaming child. The real self came to the surface under the rain of bombs. All the trivialities which often create a bad atmosphere on a ship disappeared; all of us were welded together into a Norwegian society which felt bound by its honor to help this panicky mass of people in their extreme danger."

18

Le Havre

BY JOHN RUDOLPH RUDZIN

My story begins back in February, 1940, when I joined a
Norwegian vessel in New York in order to help win the victory
for England and for France.

It was a foggy and chilly morning when we left Staten
Island. I stood on deck and recognized the Statue of Liberty
and wondered if I would see it again. This was war and many
ships never returned. Our ship went up to Canada, where we
joined a big convoy and shortly afterward started for Europe.
The sea was very rough, as it usually is in the North Atlantic
in winter. Orders were to keep a certain speed, but our ship
was an old coal burner and when we got into a gale in the
middle of the Atlantic we fell out of convoy. It was a terrible
feeling for all of us. To go in a convoy is one thing, but to
go alone in waters swarming with enemy ships is quite another. The ship was heavily loaded; even on deck there were
army trucks. As fireman I worked far below the waterline. If
any torpedo struck, I knew I would be the first to disappear
from this world. Still we didn't hesitate, because we knew
that even if anything happened, we were doing a good work.
And our faith and luck never failed us. After twenty-two
days we reached our destination, Le Havre in Free France,

early in March. At that time Le Havre was not yet being bombed and we got a nice rest while the cargo was being unloaded. After some weeks we left Le Havre en route to England and Norway, after which we were to return to New York for new cargo. But we didn't know the fate that awaited us.

We arrived at Swansea, an English port west on the Bristol Channel. We took on a cargo of coal for Norway and as before traveled alone up the east coast of England to Kirkwall, north of Scotland, where we joined a convoy for Norway.

Early on April 9 we sighted the Norwegian coast. The day began sunny and we were all excited, especially the Norwegians who had not been home for a long time and were now returning with gifts from many foreign lands for their sweethearts, sisters, and brothers. Everyone was in high spirits. Then something happened. Up went the ship's war flags and the whole convoy was ordered to turn back. What happened nobody knew at the time. But we turned back. We started guessing that perhaps something was wrong in Norway. None of the poor Norwegian boys knew that they had already lost their country, their loved ones, and all that was nearest and dearest to them. We found out when we returned to England.

Now our ship was no longer "neutral." It was in the terrible war and everyone on board became the bitterest enemy of the Nazis. Once again we had been lucky not to fall into Nazi hands—had missed it by only a few hours—and were still free to fight the bitterest enemies the world ever had.

After that we went into the port of Newcastle on the east coast of Scotland [*sic*], where we repainted our ship and put an anti-magnetic cable around her for protection against magnetic mines. Then we sailed in convoy along the east coast of England. There I got my first real taste of war. The weather was nice, the sun shining, and everything was quiet. Then suddenly—bang! a couple of feet from our ship a column of water spouted high, water dashed over our ship, and our ship was terribly shaken. More bombs! And then we saw black planes high up in the blue skies. The Germans were experts. We put on life belts and stood by the lifeboats, but you can imagine staying on an open deck with no place to escape, and seeing nothing but water all around and bombs dropping from above. I think I will never forget that. No bomb hit the convoy, and it wasn't more than a couple of minutes before English pursuit planes flew in and a terrible air battle began high over our heads. Two Nazi planes were shot down and others managed to escape, but they too were caught and brought down, as we afterwards learned. Some Nazi pilots parachuted out of their planes and were picked up by warships. After that everything was calm. It seemed the Germans didn't take more risks. They had got what they asked for!

So we went to Le Havre with the coal that we had intended for Norway. We circled England, up the west coast and down the east. As we passed Dover on our way to France, we heard a terrible booming in the direction of Holland. This was the time when Holland was being invaded by the Germans.

There was never again a nice, quiet time in Le Havre. The Germans pressed in on the city from the east and north. Every night they started bombing at ten o'clock and kept it up until four in the morning. And such bombing! As many as a hundred planes came at a time and bombed everything—houses, civilians, docks, stations, ships. That was the toughest time of my life. One day in June a rumor came that the Germans planned to wipe out the town. At the same time we got an order to be on board ship at ten o'clock that night. I came aboard at ten and had scarcely arrived when hell broke loose. How many planes were overhead we didn't know, but there were many hundreds of them.

A terrible racket started; all kinds of anti-aircraft went into action. There were bomb explosions burning ships and gasoline tanks. It was getting light as day. Planes came down on fire and many German planes exploded in midair when they hit balloon traps. We all stood in our rooms holding each other's hands. Some started to cry, some prayed. And then another bomb would whistle right over our heads and we felt it would hit us and we put our hands over our faces. Then more terrible explosions came, one by one in split seconds. The air pressure threw everyone down. Water rushed in over the ship, wreckage fell, powder smoke was everywhere, and the ship listed. "Now we got it! Now we got it!" we cried bewildered and grabbed life belts. We thought the ship would go down. But when we jumped on deck—wonder of wonders! the ship stayed as before, only there was a big mess of wreckage around us—big stones, deck cargo, debris all over. As we learned later, two bombs were intended for our ship, but both of them missed us by inches: one fell into the water alongside us and the other blew up a whole freight house on the dock and made a great hole in the ground. We escaped death by a miracle! It was a terrible night, this night when the Germans had vowed to wipe out Le Havre. They had already begun surrounding the city and our ship was ordered to take all silver, silks, and anything that was valuable out of Le Havre.

Gloomy days began in what had always been a merry city. Homes were burned, shops were closed, people packed their belongings, women and children wept, many innocent people were killed. The deadly Nazi hand reached the town and all Free French peoples.

Sunday morning. Another sleepless night after a terrible bombing. I came on deck. Strange that it was day, yet dark as night. Then we learned why—Le Havre had been evacuated. The people had been ordered to leave town under cover of the smoke screen from the blowing up of gasoline tanks.

The Germans had closed practically all the roads that led out of town, but they had left some ships, among them ours. We got orders to leave at once.

People were panic-stricken; everyone rushed to the ships which had been left. All day long half-crazed civilians came aboard our ship—crying women, children, old men, without baggage, without a bite of food, just to save their lives from the Nazis. Our ship was an old tramp with no comforts. People filled the cargo rooms, the bunkers, and all our rooms. We had no place for any more, and thousands still waited on shore. By nightfall we had fifteen hundred refugees and escapees from Le Havre.

We left in darkness and horror, without protection. The English Channel was full of enemy submarines and mines. There were hundreds of women and children on board and we had no life belts for them—only a couple of lifeboats which could at best save a hundred if anything happened. But what of the rest of the fifteen hundred? We didn't dare to think about it. We staked everything on chance, prayed to God to be with us this time when we were trying to save so many lives. Most of the people got nothing to eat and they slept on deck or inside wherever they got a place. We seamen gave our bunks to sick women and children and our meals to everyone. Of course, that was not enough for so many people, but we did what we could. We slept where we worked—firemen in the coal bunkers, sailors beside the wheel. But we were happy because we were saving the lives of many innocent people. We were doing a great work and we were proud of that.

Some went crazy on board, crazy from the awfulness of what they had seen in the evacuated town. Some mothers had lost their children and children had lost their mothers. My pen cannot describe all the horrors I saw.

But we were lucky. We reached Cherbourg, and our refugees were saved. They left Cherbourg and went into the interior of France where they were safe from Nazis.

Before they left the ship, they couldn't find words enough with which to thank us, they were so glad. They took up a collection of fifty thousand francs to pay us for the favor, but we gave the money to the French Red Cross in further aid to the poor people.

Then we went to Bordeaux (all the time without convoy) for more cargo, since we hadn't got a full cargo at Le Havre. There we didn't get in because the town was already surrounded by Germans. We lay at anchor outside and waited for orders. Our first order was to load full up in Bordeaux and then go to New York. We didn't know what to do.

The place where we lay was also bombarded by the Germans. At night they dropped magnetic mines by parachute; in the daytime, bombs. We didn't fear the magnetic mines because we had anti-magnetic cables around the ship, but we did fear the bombs. Our ship was really a lucky ship! We suffered no harm, though British ships went down right and left. After some days we got orders to go away to Casablanca, because the Germans had alreay come to Bordeaux; so again we escaped from the Nazis by the skin of our teeth.

19

In Brest

LETTER BY TORWALD MESSEL
Captain of the S.S. *Ringulv*

Casablanca
September 15, 1940

Mr. Tellef Stendal
New York City

DEAR COUSIN:

It was good to see you again after such a long time. I hope that all is well with you and your family as well as with Christian's.

You certainly were in luck to get your family back to the States at the very last moment. It must have been terrible in Norway after the German occupation. Destiny was with us too when we did not get there. After the unloading in Le Havre we were delayed for a time in order to have some damage repaired which we had suffered in crossing. From there we went to Swansea and took on cargo for Oslo. Within four hours of Norwegian waters our convoy was turned back. No one knew why, and about half the ships had gone on and arrived in Norway, as we heard. Later the story came over the radio. You know what it was. We were taken to England,

first to one port and then to another, where together with
sixty other Norwegian vessels we waited for three weeks. Then
we got orders to deliver a cargo of coal to Le Havre. In Tyne
we had an electric cable laid around the ship to protect it
against magnetic mines, and that took a week. We passed
the south coast of England on the day the Germans invaded
Holland and Belgium. We were bombed several times along
the English coast and saw some dramatic air fights. Two
planes were shot down, and the crews bailed out in parachutes
and were taken up by the escort. We stayed in Le Havre until
June 10. After we had unloaded the coal, we began loading
for the United States. But the loading was stopped, and we
were ordered to take refugees on board. We took on fifteen
hundred of them and proceeded to Cherbourg. There we
were ordered to continue to Brest. Before we could leave, we
had to get fresh water and provisions, since we had neither
on board and the refugees had brought nothing with them.
About half of the refugees were women and children, many
of them babies, one only two days old. There were also a
number who were ill and some invalids, but fortunately we
had a Red Cross nurse and several others who knew something about nursing.

We turned over to them everything we had of cabins,
salons, and messes. The cabins of the officers and the crew
were overcrowded. The mates and I slept on the floor of the
radio room when we were not on the bridge. I had to be up
there almost all the time, since we ran into heavy fog near
the Guernsey Islands. The table in the salon was put lengthwise along the starboard side, and that was full of babies. We
gave away our supplies of preserved milk, bread, jam, coffee,
tea, etc. The cook baked as fast as he could, but it was little
for so many. However, we got along.

We arrived at Brest on the afternoon of June 13, with
everything in fine order for the debarkation. We put to along-

side the wharf and used a broad gangway which they supplied us from shore. There were Red Cross nurses with a soup canteen, Boy and Girl Scout assistants, and guards. The authorities of town and port and of the Navy came down to welcome the refugees. Big buses and trucks carried them up into the city after they had been divided into groups. Before they disembarked, we received a nice letter of thanks signed by their leader, a colonel, and by the leader of each single group. Under the initiative of the Red Cross nurse and her aids the refugees collected some money to give us as a gift. In all it amounted to 1,500 francs. I said that we could not accept anything, but they insisted; I then suggested that we donate the gift to the French Red Cross, and everybody agreed. This was told to the refugees in a speech by the colonel, first on the foredeck and later on boat deck. There were great ovations and much applause and shouting, "Vive la Norvège."

The debarkation went quickly and easily; two officers at the gangway checked passports and two of our crew stood guard, one on each side. After two hours the people and their luggage had been landed, and we were shifted to the roadstead. About one thousand people were still on the pier waving to us and shouting hooray.

The Norwegian consul at Le Havre accompanied us to the Verdun Roads, where we had received orders to go on the following day. We were to have gone to Bordeaux but never got beyond the Verdun Roads until June 20, when we received orders to go to Casablanca. We came here June 25 and have discharged some of the cargo consigned to Bordeaux, but we still have the U.S. cargo on board. We probably will be laid up here for the duration.

From May 21 until we left Le Havre on June 10 we were under heavy bombing almost incessantly, day and night, and had to stick to the air-raid shelters during the attacks. They started almost precisely at 9:45 every night and kept on until one or two o'clock in the morning. We had more than one narrow escape. Bombs fell close to the ship, on the quay, or on the dock, so that huge stones flew into the water and sent it sky-high on the ship. The whole ship got black from powder and smoke, and from the muddy water on the docks. One night both lamps in the salons were thrown off their hooks, where they had hung through the worst of weathers. They fell on the table, and china, glass, and paraffin flew everywhere. If one went to town during the day, there were air alarms every now and then, so one had to take to the shelters to be protected against the hail of splinters, which were the most dangerous of all. The anti-air barrage was excellent and many planes were shot down day and night; the devastation in the town itself was therefore smaller than might have been expected. We thought we were through with the bombing when we left Le Havre, but the Germans advanced quickly and took that city on June 13. They were not far away when we reached the Verdun Roads and began bombing the very first night. They came back regularly day and night and dropped bombs and electric mines in parachutes; we could watch them from the ship. We saw no damage done but were told that a ship ran against an electric mine not far away. So we started degaussing. We have certainly had enough of this war and hope it will soon be over.

20

A Country Lad at Sea

BY NIELS TJELMELAND

My kinsman Tolleiv was only a little fellow the last time I saw him, about twenty years ago. I see him yet as he stood there in the middle of a green meadow, scythe in hand, barefoot, bareheaded, his pants hanging by one suspender strap. The legs of the pants seemed fearfully long, dangled halfway to his ankles, one leg longer than the other.

It was a warm afternoon of early summer. The encircling mountains slumbered in a blue haze and their slopes were clothed in their freshest green. The long dwellings, their windows glittering, lay gray in the sunlight. The song of a mowing machine reached me from a patch of meadow to the south. Up on the slopes a cowbell tinkled—in single clunks; a cow lay chewing her cud and for the sake of peace chasing a fly from her muzzle. Far below through a cleft I could see a strip of the fjord, where the water was calm as glass.

And in the midst of all this grandeur stood the little boy with the scythe in his hand. He was going to be a farmer like his father and his grandfather before him. This was, as I said, twenty years ago. No one dreamed then what the next twenty years would bring.

But during those twenty years Tolleiv became a man, and

it was as such that I met him again in New York a short time
ago. He had become a seaman, a tall, slender seaman, wearing
the uniform of the Royal Norwegian Navy. He told me his
story, which I now repeat.

"I was at home in K—— working as a carpenter when I
received my mobilization order on the fifth of April, 1940—
four days before the fateful ninth. I was sent to Horten and
assigned to a destroyer, and I stayed with that ship until the
fighting was over in Norway. Then we set out for England,
where the King and Government had gone and from where
the war was to be continued. I might say too that before we
left we had had a chance to make ourselves useful in Norway
by sinking a German troop transport outside of Haugesund.

"In England I applied for admission to the merchant
marine and was accepted. I became cannoneer on a cargo
vessel. Our first job was to evacuate British troops from Dunkirk. It was no fun. Under a rain of bombs we steamed out
of the harbor, loaded with troops. Luck was, however, with
us, though others were not so lucky. At least fifteen ships
nearby were sunk and the sea was full of men who swam and
splashed and went under. The harbor looked like a sea of
spouting fountains. We made only the one trip there.

"Later our ship sailed between London and New York.
Once, early in 1941, we were surprised about three hundred
miles off New York by the big German battleship *Scharnhorst,* which put a prize crew on board our ship. The trip from
our ship to the *Scharnhorst* was far from comfortable. The sea
was so rough it was simply impossible to let down a boat, and
we were pulled through the waves by a rope. Our captain, an
elderly man, got rough treatment; he couldn't brace himself
against the side of the ship and was thoroughly shaken up. I
had a tooth knocked out.

"On board the battleship I was separated from the captain.
He was taken to a cabin. I was sent down into the hold,

where there already were about five hundred English prisoners. It was so crowded that there was hardly room to lie down. I slept in a hammock hung at the foot of a stairway and lay curled up like a pretzel. The food we got consisted of thin macaroni soup and nothing else.

"I shall never forget these four days we were aboard and sat shivering down at the bottom of that floating hell. The battleship was in action many times. We did not know what was going on. We had only one wish and that was that an Allied warship would sink us. We knew what our fate would be, and still we wished it with all our hearts.

"The *Scharnhorst* put us ashore at Brest. From there we were transported to a prison camp nearby, where we were kept for two weeks. The most peculiar thing about this stay was that while Brest was blacked out every night, our camp was lighted with every light it had. The object of this was to mislead English planes coming over into hitting us instead of the Germans. They came over Brest several times during those two weeks, but a bomb never fell near our prison camp. They knew how to find their targets in spite of the Germans' tricks.

"We were then sent through France, Belgium, and Holland to Hamburg, and put in another prison camp, where there already were several hundred Norwegians—whalers who had fallen into the hands of the Germans. They were now going to be sent to Norway. We did not know where we were to be sent—some had heard that it was to a prison camp in the interior of Germany. I talked with some of the prisoners from the whaling fleet, and they said they were going home very soon. This gave me an idea. I had no desire to sit imprisoned in Germany for the duration, so one night when all the lights were out I picked up my bedding and trudged over to one of the barracks where the whalers were. I found an empty cot and threw myself down on it. It was none too soon. When we were lined up for inspection the next morning, I was not recognized, and heard that the Norwegian prisoners were to embark for Norway that very day.

"When we reached Oslo, thousands of people were at the pier. The quislings had been diligent in publicizing Hitler's magnanimity, and now the Norwegians were to see it with their own eyes. The whalers were coming home!

"The quislings, on hand with orators and fanfare, were certain that this was their big day. But the whalers stood silent at the rails with bowed heads. It was good to see Norway again—but it was also depressing. They knew that Norway was no longer free.

"I was at home for a few days and in that time I discovered that there was not a single quisling in my parish. Of course, the parish is not so big. All told there are perhaps not more than twenty farmers in it, and still the Germans had found it necessary to station a whole company of soldiers there. They marched back and forth on the country road, clicking their heels and irritating the farmers no end with their ridiculous goose-stepping.

"After I had rested a little and talked with people, I went back to K——, where I got carpenter work again. But it was not to last long. The Norwegians had sent me to Horten to become a seaman; the Germans, who discovered that I was also a carpenter, decided to allow me to continue in that trade, which was not so bad. But the place and the work did not suit me. When I received a letter one morning ordering me to report at T—— for work on the Murmansk front building fortifications—civilian conscription, they called it—I had no doubts about what I would do. Through friends I had got word of a fishing smack which was setting out across the North Sea from the vicinity of Haugesund.

"I hopped on my bicycle and rode home the same day. There I got together some clothes and told my sister that I would be back in a few hours. Instead I took the bus to Haugesund and contacted those who were leaving. Fortunately I knew a couple of them and when I told my story they let me come along. There were thirty of us in all.

"At twilight we went out on the fjord, cast nets, and acted as if we were fishing. The German patrol planes, which occasionally flew overhead, took us for fishermen and continued on their way. By eleven o'clock it was sufficiently dark and we hoisted the Norwegian flag, started the motor, and with our course set for England, headed out to sea. We landed in Scotland and got a royal welcome from the hospitable Scots.

"In England I signed on a Norwegian freighter again, as cannoneer this time too. We went westward to America and from there east to Singapore. It was perilous in Singapore during those days because the Japs were bombing it. From Singapore we went to Durban in South Africa, and from Durban to India. There I became ill and was sent to the hospital in Karachi. After that I went aboard a new ship bound for the States, but became ill again. It's a nervous stomach condition."

Here Tolleiv's story ends. He is now preparing to go to England. He is nervous and not well, and has lost about sixty pounds. But he will keep on sailing until Norway is free again. He never thought he would become a seaman, but he does his duty—a seafaring country lad.

Coastal Africa and the Mediterranean

~~~~~~~~~~~~~~~~~~~~~~~~~~~~~~

21

One Year Aboard the Troopship "Bergensfjord"

BY SVERRE KNOPF

December 19, 1940. Liverpool. Today the interior of the *Bergensfjord*—lounges, third-class quarters, etc.—is being torn out to make place for the accommodation of 2,000 troops.

December 20–21. Air-raid alarm at 6:40 P.M. and continuous bombing of city until 4:00 A.M. Huge fires in warehouses and on the docks all around us. Hell unimaginable. All men below deck up all night waiting. Machine-gun and cannon fire and bomb explosions drown each other out. Many fires in the city. Many houses destroyed. Docks littered with debris, splinters, rubble from incendiary bombs and exploded land mines.

December 27. Liverpool. Carpenters putting up bunks on the sun decks on both starboard and port sides looking toward the bow right in front of my cabin. What a beautiful mess this will be night and day. It is said that we will be going on a long voyage to the tropics—a trip of some 7 to 13 weeks. No air attack today, luckily.

December 28. Dinner at the Hotel Adelphi. This hotel, the city's finest and largest, badly battered by bombing these past days and has just managed to keep going with 40 beds instead of 350.

December 29. Englishmen at work all over the ship, which will soon be unrecognizable.

January 4, 1941. Cold, heavy air has hung over the city, so Jerry has not shown up for several days. Danger signals continuing now and then nonetheless. Our crew made up of many nationalities. The deck patrol calls us the League of Nations.

January 11–14. Work on the big remodeling goes forward under the deafening din of bombing and anti-aircraft fire. The stokehole is made over for food storage.

January 20. Took on and enrolled 21 men from the *Oslo-fjord,* which was torpedoed outside of Newcastle about a month ago. Work on alterations continues both inside and out. Constructing paravanes and setting up extra anti-aircraft.

February 2. Left Liverpool 11:45. Some troops on board; some crews outdistanced. Large convoy arrived today. Several troopships left simultaneously with us; to meet us in Glasgow. Belgians, French, and British.

February 3. Sailed along the west coast of Scotland; enter the firth this morning. More than 120 ships of all classes large and small lie here. Nature beautiful. Resembles the entrance to a city like Bergen. Proceed to Glasgow, sail up the Clyde, pass numerous shipyards, big and small, among them John Brown's, where the *Queen Mary* and the *Queen Elizabeth* were built. An enormous number of ships under construction.

February 4. Glasgow. Immigration officers check the whole crew. 230 soldiers on board. Fine fellows in full field attire and pith helmets.

February 5. Glasgow. Embarkation of troops completed. Much excitement on board. An ant hill. Bunks everywhere.

Duffel bags, clothing, hammocks, food containers from floor to ceiling, tables, benches. Soldiers pack the enormous rooms on the two lower decks which now occupy the entire area where the cabins were torn out. We are now a troopship loaded to capacity. The galley mess crew is working like crazy and I don't see how they can keep up this rush for the 30–40 days the trip is expected to take. 1,200 kg. [about 2,640 lb.] of meat have been consumed today; 20 sacks of potatoes; several sacks of cabbage and other vegetables, etc. Looks as if it were a matter of life and death. I dread what will happen when we reach the warmer latitudes.

February 6. Left Glasgow about 4:00 P.M. with 1,904 troops. A strange departure from a cold, gray dock. No "Yes, we love with fond devotion"; dead silence; no music; no one to see anyone off; no waving of white handkerchiefs; no flowers and serpentines. But the *Bergensfjord* glides proudly down the Clyde crammed with troops, and the Norwegian split flag flying high on the rear spar, waving briskly and proudly in every direction as we pass all the large shipyards at slow speed. All the berths on both sides are full of ship hulls. Workmen by the thousands wave to our troops and exchange shouts with them. All men wearing life belts. All troops are in high spirits this evening, ale flowing generously. There is song and music. Life swarms everywhere. We await order for departure.

February 8. Leave for an unknown port. The great moment has come when the whole convoy sets out to sea, and we can now expect an attack by the enemy at any moment— U-boat or plane. Everyone is at his station at the cannons and machine guns. The captain, mates, signalmen, marine officers, are on the bridge and a man is in the crow's nest. Ship's papers and other valuable documents are in waterproof bags; life preservers, hatchets, and waterproof flashlights in readiness in the cabins.

February 9. Our 12 troopships and 30 cargo ships are protected by two light cruisers and 12 larger and smaller torpedo boats. We are traveling in a broad convoy at a speed of 9 knots. A slight sea and cold. Soldiers and officers are very forthright and friendly. The common soldiers have to wash, scrub, and carry food for the officers, and queue up for chow themselves.

February 10. High seas and much seasickness among the boys. They lie prone all over the ship, including in front of my door day and night so I can hardly get in or out. They look miserable. Large British planes on patrol today. We are making good headway.

February 11. Storm from the west, much seasickness among the troops. Everything rattles and slides. High seas and low visibility should lessen the fear of any attack. Ships heaving and tossing. It's a sight to see the whole convoy breaking its way through the sea spray. A few depth mines were dropped during the day. U-boats suspected in the area.

February 13. Report of a German raider attack and a ship sunk off the coast of Portugal. Changed course to due north because of the risk.

February 15. At 11:00 A.M. met by the battleship *Rodney,* a 42,000-tonner with 16-inch cannons. She is to escort us southward for a few days until we meet new relief. This evening I was in the company of the English Captain Arnot, who disclosed that in the blockades of both the previous war and the present one in 1939 *he* had pursued and seized the *Bergensfjord.* He now thought it bizarre that he should be standing on our captain's bridge to protect and help the *Bergensfjord* against an enemy. Today, in other words, the situation was reversed: he was himself the pursued and the *Bergensfjord* his friend and helper.

February 16. Fair weather, all's well. Big concert by military band and other performers. It's hard on the beer and cigarettes, and the smoke smell hangs heavy everywhere because the whole ship is practically closed up tight under the blackout.

February 17. Today gunnery practice and old *Bergensfjord* shakes to her foundations. Planes whirr all over the horizon. We are accompanied by the warship *Renown* and the airplane carrier *Ark Royal*—fine stuff. Everyone is beginning to feel at home on board. A good feeling and atmosphere dominate. The food is liked and everything is satisfactory—it's only that it is pretty crowded.

February 22. The troops have daily calisthenics on deck, tugs of war and deck hockey. Strong, fine young fellows all of them. An astonishing spirit of congeniality among them. One gets absolutely no impression of fear or anxiety about the horrors which await them. On the contrary there is laughter, singing, and downright jesting, a wholesomeness about all of them.

February 24–25. Warmer. Troops now wear khaki, shorts, and pith helmets; awnings cover the entire deck both aft and fore where boxing exhibitions and deck games take place. We now have four or five destroyers guarding us, since U-boats are feared. U-boats in the vicinity sighted and chased.

March 2. Arrived Freetown (Sierra Leone) this morning. An enormous number of boats riding in the harbor and the tropical landscape is incredibly beautiful—from a distance. The natives crowd around our ship in their long, narrow, homemade boats, sell fruit and souvenirs. duck for coins, and argue with the troops who line the side railings of the ship.

March 4. Freetown a strangely romantic and idyllic tropical city of about 40,000 inhabitants, 500 of them whites. The city teems with British soldiers and marines, along with some French. Negro boys and girls speak to us constantly, beg and offer themselves for all sorts of things. Sweat streams all day long. Darkness falls suddenly around eight o'clock, but beautiful moonlight follows in a completely star-sown sky.

March 9. Left Freetown at 3:30 P.M. Zambo had a busy day selling fruit, and the jabber, selling, and hawking went on at a lively pace on both sides of the ship. There are now about 40 ships in convoy. Frightfully hot, day and night. Impossible to get anything cold to drink. Fruit and vegetables not to be had any more—only oranges now and then. As many persons as can, sleep on deck and lie strewn about like flies. Blackout every night.

March 11. Crossed the equator during the afternoon. Two thousand initiated with great ceremony into the Order of the Shellbacks, the Ancient Order of the Deep, King Neptune leading the procession. The "Central Police" made the rounds of the whole ship and those who had tried to escape the ceremonies were in for an extra dose of punishment. . . . The heat plagues day and night.

March 21. Arriving Cape Town; all quiet. Immigration officers and doctors first-rate, so we had no trouble. Customs officers not around. Loading provisions, water, oil on board all night long in order to proceed as quickly as possible in the morning.

March 22. Left Cape Town.

March 23. Sunday. We round the Cape of Good Hope. Weather delightful, temperature moderate—one senses the approach of tropical heat. Worship services at hatch number 4.

March 24. Soldier's life as usual on board with whistling and singing outside. Some wrangling going on among troops and officers. War mentality? The kitchen is a madhouse for the cooks. It will have to give sometime.

March 26. Arrived Durban about 9:30 A.M. Many other troopships arrive at the same time. Durban an ultramodern city, idyllic and inviting with fine parks and beautiful palms, fine buildings, and more attractive architecture than that of modern Oslo. A Norwegian architect did much of the building here. There are about 18,000 soldiers here of many nationalities—Indians, etc. Elegant shops, hotels, restaurants. Attended a propaganda meeting in Town Hall, where among others a German clergyman talked against Hitler and Nazism. Seven Allied nations displayed flags, and a large orchestra played "Yes, we love with fond devotion."

March 31. All troops must be on board by 6:30 P.M. for early departure tomorrow. The British military forces are doing magnificently in Eritrea and the Mediterranean and getting things in fine shape for "Mussie" when he shows up. Extensive preparations are under way for meeting the Nazi rabble in the Balkans and we are one of the forces now coming north. We are taking an enormous amount of cargo, tin among other things marked for "Turkey." Likewise enormous supplies of all kinds of food, meat, fruits and vegetables, so that *Bergensfjord* is now loaded to the waterline.

April 1. Left Durban 8:30 A.M. People saluted us along the whole harbor; "Good Luck" chalked in big letters on a huge locomotive on one of the spurs in the harbor. There is a scorching sun. We are all out of beer and have no more than a ten-day supply of mineral water. The ship is getting dirty both inside and out. The white paint, carpets, curtains, have taken fearful abuse.

April 4. Now entering the Mozambique Channel between Madagascar and East Africa, about 21 degrees south. It's dreadful for the cooks in front of the kitchen ranges, but they are taking it with remarkable composure, uncomplainingly. A lot of sweat must be dripping into the soup kettles and the skillets. Incredible that they can endure it. Germans reported to have occupied Benghazi today, and our superheated ant hill is now approaching "portal of hell" entrance to the Red Sea for a brief call at Aden.

April 11. This is Good Friday. No different from any other day on board. We are at war and are nearing the danger zone. Met a number of large liners returning southward.

April 13. Easter Sunday, Warm weather. Calm, fine sea. Under constant guard of two cruisers—*Warspite* and *Glasgow*, both of which have been in Narvik and have stirred things up in that place. Our whole ship reeks of food, swill, and brown bodies. We speed up for Aden, where we expect to be Tuesday morning.

April 15. Arrived Aden (Arabia) 8:10 A.M. and anchored in the harbor. Brought mail and telegrams to shore. Aden an Arabian desert town, ash-dry, with old, dreadful stone houses and bazaars. Goats, camels, and beggars having children with them fill the narrow streets. A poor, miserable place. Principally of military importance and well fortified. Vast stretches of salt dunes and plains toward the north and high mountains toward the south. Oil and coal depots. We take on oil, fresh water, and ice.

April 16. Left Aden at 7:00 A.M. The machinery has now, one might say, been running constantly for 53 days with no possibility of repairs or maintenance and the engineer fears that any number of things within the mechanics could give way at any time. The insulation in the electrical system and motors can be expected to melt because of the terrible heat in the engine room—between 50° and 60° C. Passed the "portal of hell" at 5:00 P.M. yesterday. Sun at the zenith. At 6:30 P.M. a starlit and tropical sky.

April 19. Packing and getting ready for debarking. Chilly, delightful weather. Farewell dinner. Passed Mount Sinai.

April 20. Arrived Suez Canal 7:00 A.M. Temp. 23° C. and we are just about freezing after having come up from the tropics. An enormous concourse of ships here. Egyptian quarantine doctors and British immigration officers came on board; had to check the crew. We are anchored in the harbor and there is a certain degree of Sunday-like peacefulness here.

April 21. The troops are now busy packing; it is almost impossible to get out anywhere on account of all kinds of truck and military equipment. Some of it will be landed this afternoon and the rest tomorrow. Situations on board hectic. From here we will probably go to Bombay or Port Sudan. Weather invigorating—chilly at 25° C. At any rate it feels chilly.

Suez. April 21. Troops landing today. They, along with their equipment, are sent ashore on large flat-bottomed barges. All are very young, upstanding fellows—they sing and are actually in fine spirits.

April 23. To shore by motorboat along with the captain. Met old Moses and his son, who speaks Norwegian. They are old and well-known ship chandlers here in Egypt, and especially well known among Norwegian seafaring folk. Suez itself is, with some exceptions, a city of more or less tumbledown hovels. Narrow streets full of small shops selling a hodgepodge from chickens and cucumbers to rags. Goats and donkeys wander in the streets and all manner of funny little shacks teem with lazy Arabs, Greeks, Assyrians, Egyptians, and children and women ragged and filthy but smiling and contented. Their garb most nearly resembles a kind of nightshirt of any conceivable make, but most of all full of dirt. And they are barefoot. It is being rumored that we are to return to England and Canada and that on our way down we are to take on Italian prisoners somewhere south of here.

April 28. Expect to take 1,700 Italian prisoners on board tomorrow; the macaroni came on board today.

April 29. Have taken on 1,700 Italian prisoners and brought them below deck. All miserably clothed, ragged and grimy with filth, but in fairly good spirits. They sang in chorus as they approached the *Bergensfjord* on tenders, and I believe they are happy to have got away from the terrors of war in the desert. For supper they were given macaroni—after bread and tea. Prisoners are not allowed to have knives or forks. They are very polite and observing and shy away if one gets near them—especially if he ranks three stripes. Among the prisoners are officers (doctors) and a small contingent of Red Cross. Indians are made use of for military surveillance and security and standing watch. There are about 130 such on board. They prepare their own food and carry on by themselves in their own strange way. Egyptian laborers unload the cargo during the day and evening; at night they lie out on deck in filth and rags. The place is a peculiar symphony of Egyptian, Italian, Scandinavian, and English tongues and song.

April 30. Left Suez 6:30 A.M. For breakfast the prisoners get oatmeal porridge, bread without butter; for dinner, coffee and a meat or fish dish.

May 1. The Indians lie outside the cabins on the sun deck and their jabber goes on night and day. On account of the blackout all portholes on the ship must be kept closed; unpleasant consequences and stench from the warmth and heat prevail accordingly.

May 5. Arrived Aden at 1:00 P.M. and anchored. Today one of the Italian prisoners died of pneumonia. Some prisoners are made use of for ship work and in reward get the same food as the crew. The way they gorge is something dreadful. They smack their lips and act like overgrown kids turned loose in a children's paradise.

May 6. Left Aden this morning. Buried the Italian who died, and the Indian soldiers marched to the sound of trumpets. The name of the deceased was Dicicco Guiseppe, 22 years. One of the Italian doctors officiated. The body, sewed in a sheet of canvas and covered with a Norwegian flag, was then lowered into the sea. Of all the Italians only about 25 displayed their allegiance in a fascist salute, which indicates that not many ally themselves with Mussolini. When we mention Mussolini and look inquiringly at them, they are quick to shake their heads in denial and show plain dissatisfaction by grimaces of contempt. They are miserably outfitted and have very little clothing or footwear.

May 8. Course due east. We are a group of four transports: *Leopoldville,* Belgian; *Scythia, Cammeronia,* and *Nova Scotia,* British. All carry Italian prisoners—between 1,800 and 2,000—with the exception of *Nova Scotia,* which has 2,000 women and children. A light cruiser escorts us. The "Dagos" had a boxing exhibition on the foredeck this morning and in other ways seem to have fun and amuse themselves with whatever they enjoy. They bum cigarettes and find use for everything of food, clothing, and tidbits they can get hold of.

May 9. Today the raider *Hansa* was sunk in the Indian Ocean not far from here by the Britisher *Cornwall.* The cruiser was one of our escorts on the way up.

May 16. Arrived Durban. Italians put ashore. Took trip to the museum and saw many interesting things—the zoological and historical sections and the art gallery, which among other things included a painting by Munch!

May 26. Today we had the historic experience of greeting 32 Norwegian boys who had fled from Norway in March and April of this year—from Oslo, Kongsvinger, Stavanger, Porsgrund, Skien, etc. Most of them escaped singly through Sweden, Russia, Roumania, Bulgaria over to and across the Black Sea, through Irak, Iran, and the Persian Gulf down to Bombay in India and from there to Durban by boat; they are bound for the Royal Norwegian Air Force in Scotland and Canada by way of Freetown. They docked alongside us and the enthusiasm over a meeting of this kind was mutual. All news from home was devoured with intense interest, and we saw more clearly all that is going on at home. The boys were invited to supper with us on board and when they were treated to Norwegian meatballs with gravy they went wild. Afterwards they were given drinks and the jabber went on until nearly midnight in warm winter moonlight.

May 27. Left Durban for Freetown at 6:30 A.M.

May 29. Now rounding the Cape of Good Hope and traveling northward. We are proceeding at full speed without escort. A little warmer. I hope Roosevelt's speech of yesterday will be especially encouraging to the people of Norway. He has now made manifest to Hitler and the Germans his and the United States' clenched fist. . . . We now have three passengers on board. Our boat looks shabby. Interior completely ruined—dingy, unpolished, neglected. Whole galley establishment has fared badly.

June 5. Arrived Victoria, formerly a German colony, at 10:00 A.M. Beautiful landscapes, at times high mountains, and then again jungle. Many sambos out in boats selling wares. Old shirts, singlets, hats, cloth rags, go like hot cakes in exchange for bananas and other fruit. Monkeys 5 to 10 shillings. Taking on cargo today—ammunition, automobiles, and various other war materials, together with about 500 black troops, 100 per cent African Negroes. Also some British officers. U-boat reported off Lagos. Bad news from Europe today.

June 6. News somewhat better. Taking on board the remaining 1,150 black troops, considerable equipment; also automobiles in transport. The troops get two meals a day—rice and meat with oil and curry. They prefer to eat sitting on the floor. They are tractable, obedient fellows and good at helping with all cleaning, washing, and polishing on board.

June 8. Muggy air, but not so suffocatingly hot. The Negro troops have calisthenics and muster on deck every day. In the evening there are all kinds of Negro dances, war dances, and tom-toms. They can play the flute and horn. We are approaching Freetown and meantime the U-boats are active in the danger zone ahead. Shooting may break loose at any time.

June 11–12. Now headed straight toward Freetown, zig-zagging like the very devil. U-boats reported nearby every day; everything in readiness.

June 13. Arrived Freetown unhindered by U-boats. Passenger ship *Ada* sunk 17 miles outside of Freetown a few days ago; 8 killed, about 400 rescued; one Norwegian cargo ship went down the same day and several were killed and drowned.

June 16. Have begun taking troops on board, about 800 today. Rain, with thunder and lightning, pours down in the evening and during the night. Large flat-bottomed, motor-propelled barges bring the transport from shore.

June 17. At the shipping commissioner's today, but no hands to be had. Unemployed crews here are quickly dispatched to England; bad climate and considerable malaria also responsible. Continue embarking troops. Having been in training here for ten months, they look a bit skinny and starved, and many have had malaria. But they sing and are in good spirits for all that.

June 20. Left Freetown 1:30 P.M. with 1,977 soldiers on board. We are in all 15 large troopships convoyed by a larger number of destroyers and cruisers.

June 21. Food stale and poor, everything tastes refrigerator. We travel at a speed of 14 knots. All ships are blacked out at night, so it is a wonder we don't collide.

July 4. Arrived Durban between 10:00 and 11:00 A.M. The other troopships in our squadron are berthed along the same quay. Everyone has shore leave. Newspapers get snapped up in a jiffy when 10,000 men all want one at once. Many soldiers come down with malaria. City teems with all kinds of soldiers in a motley array of uniforms.

July 6. Visited the *Mauretania* and the *Samaria* in dock back of us and had a look at their interiors. Very elegant and solidly constructed throughout. No German ersatz. Practically nothing on board is what one might call damaged, but temporary bunks have been installed in all of the otherwise large and roomy cabins, and in the lounges and other open places as well.

July 7. The crew has collected £255 sterling to be turned over to the consulate as a contribution to the Submarine Chaser Fund in London.

July 13. Arrived Cape Town. Called at the Norwegian Society and the Seamen's House and met genial hosts. Two Norwegian flags waved outside the buildings. The quarters are very attractive. Walls adorned with Norwegian pictures.

July 18. Walvis Bay. Arrived 8:00 A.M. A God-forsaken place of extensive stretches of sand and squat houses, but with railroad connections. In peacetime an old shore station during the whaling season. Take on cargo of dried hides and manganese, also canned crab. Crew of mixed nationalities. Proceed without escort to Trinidad.

July 29–30. Saw a suspicious-looking ship on the horizon. Changed course immediately and got out of the way with a fanfare. Passed a deal of wreckage, a raft, boxes, and other flotsam and jetsam, presumably from a ship which had been sunk.

August 2. Arrived Trinidad. Trinidad a beautiful place with lots of pretty trees, palms, green shrubbery, flowers. Brought mail to shore.

August 3. Left for Halifax.

August 30. Glasgow. Norwegian fishing smacks chug back and forth in the harbor. These have stolen out of Norway and do duty in various ways here. Some of them have been stolen back from the Germans filled with food and oil and have come across.

September 13. As we glide out the Clyde we pass the *Empress of Canada,* which had just brought the Svalbard colony to Glasgow. Contact with them was not permitted.

September 15. Today we are listening to Prime Minister Nygaardsvold's speech with its encouraging assurance that something is about to happen. There will be a good house-cleaning and the Nazis will have to pay for their sins. We who are aboard the *Bergensfjord* are ready to take whatever it may be; we know what has been going on at home and what our dear ones in Norway are suffering. We burn for the chance to chase the devils out and bring deliverance.

September 16. British marines on board today. Orders to sail. Troops to Iceland. Embarkation begins tomorrow. Everything is made ready for clearing.

September 17. Greenock. About 150 marines on board today. The whole ship is in a flurry of activity, to take on more troops tomorrow and leave immediately. A troupe of performers, men and women, will go with us to entertain British and American troops in Iceland.

September 18. Left Greenock at 10:40 P.M. after the last of the troops had been taken on board. Escorted by two destroyers, proceeding smoothly; everything in fine order. We are now conditioned for everything. Anti-aircraft and watch on all over the ship. Three sled dogs from Svalbard keep up their kind of racket on the sun deck and the stench of dog ordure hangs over half the ship. There are also four puppies.

September 21. Arrived Reykjavik harbor, and ride at anchor far out after having played hawk and dove with U-boats all the way up. There are British, American, and Norwegian troops on the island. Foul weather today, with cold, rain, and wind. Many ships at anchor out here—Norwegian ones and a number of Norwegian fishing smacks which have fled here. Some of the British military officers have Norwegian wives and speak a very good Norwegian.

September 22. Brought troops and shipwrecked seamen on board, about 2,500 altogether. Storm in the harbor. Have had

visits from several Norwegians here. Song and music. Whol
ship swarms with soldiers; jammed to the stacks—a hell of
turmoil everywhere.

September 23. At sea. Bound for England. Carrying witl
us the surviving crews of 14 or 18 torpedoed ships of al
nationalities. Flags of Panama, England, Holland, Sweden
The seamen include all sorts of Allied nations. Among th
passengers are 250 Faroese and a number of German wa
prisoners from disabled U-boats. Twenty-one-year-olds all c
them; the eldest, the commander, is 27. They are held unde
arrest under strong guard. The office staff is working at whit
heat on lists, manifestoes, and all kinds of military papers
We have a Norwegian flight captain on board, a Captain W
a very forthright, genial fellow who has a good deal of in
teresting information on conditions in Iceland and elsewhere
Also knows the latest news from Norway. Fled from there i
March.

October 5. Reykjavik again. Visit from nurses Marit an
Kaia, who have just come up here from England on the *Lyr*
Had a little party up at Captain Velle's, where I also met Cap
tain Ulring, chief of the *Sleipner,* and had a very pleasar
and interesting conversation with him about actual militar
matters. He could give a very considerable account of hi
military expeditions at home. The town was full of Yankee:
British and American uniforms. The stir of great busyness in
different world prevailed on both harbor and land. Visite
the Norwegian air base.

October 7. At sea. Hear SOS from a Norwegian boa
which has been torpedoed close by but is afloat and sets
course for Iceland.

October 15. Was surprised to find Callin Petch sudden
confronting me as a British soldier. Petch is the son of ou
well-known radio announcer Gladys Petch, both of whom
learned to know as fellow workers in N.A.L. and at the Ber

nett Travel Bureau. The sirens are screaming and danger signals are being tested. Rain and foul weather.

November 5. Glasgow. I had brought with me the records and cash balance which, during my stay in London, had been left for safekeeping at the office in Glasgow. At the gangplank I handed these valuable papers and the money, sealed in a thick, large envelope, to the quartermaster, who took them. In the very instant that I myself jumped in good style and safely on board, I saw the quartermaster drop the packet, which fell straight into the ocean. Among other things it contained $1,300 and several hundred pounds sterling. I leaped resolutely into the water with all my clothes on—hat and coat —and retrieved the packet at the very last instant. I was pulled up into the motorboat with great difficulty and had to trudge about on board drenched to the skin and had to change all my clothes. But my honor was preserved and I was the hero of the day. (Later got into the Scots' newspapers on account of it.)

December 3. A visit on board by members of the Defense Department. A collection of men's clothing and accessories now in progress on board to be smuggled in one way or other into Norway. I gave two pair of pants, all I own of shirts and underwear, together with some home-knit socks which Mother had made. I parted with them with a certain feeling of piety. But—all for Norway!

December 22. We are to leave at 2:00 P.M., and embarkation is to begin early. The situations on board are altogether hectic. We have all sorts of people—about 30 Russians, 100 Americans, many Canadians and Newfoundlanders. Women and children, in addition to about 2,000 troops, mostly from the Air Force, who are to train in Canada, together with seamen for ships in the U.S.A.

December 26. The ship is a sizzling witch's cauldron. No Christmas tree, no lights, no song, no music. We have rice porridge with fruit juice and rib roast for supper. The troops and certain of their officers regale themselves with beer. A struggle to make lists of troops and passengers. There are 222 civilians, among them Professor Charles H. Best, the discoverer of insulin. Blackout and closed ventilators make the air inside bad and oppressive.

New Year's Eve. We travel at slow speed and are to be in at 5:00 A.M. tomorrow. Today the spirit on board is fine; all feel safe and most of them celebrate. We have a delicious dinner of soup, fish, ribs with ale. I am wondering all the while what they are having at home today. Bitterly cold, but a calm sea.

[Excerpts from his daybook.]

22

The M.S. "Thermopylae"

I

In the spring of 1940 when the Germans invaded Norway, a number of young Norwegians were studying in Switzerland, particularly in Zurich. Among them was Arne B. Knudsen, an ensign in the Norwegian military engineer service, who believed that he might be of use to his country somewhere. Together with ten comrades he traveled through France, and was caught there at the time of the French collapse. In Bordeaux, as a student of radio engineering, he signed up as a telegrapher on an old Norwegian vessel, the M.S. *Ledaal,* and reached the ship at the very last moment she could escape from the Germans. After a call at England the *Ledaal* crossed the Atlantic. In Philadelphia, Knudsen signed up as telegrapher on the M.S. *Thermopylae,* under Captain Carl Thorleif Corneliussen. Ensign Knudsen is here interviewed on the story of the *Thermopylae.*

The *Thermopylae* had already been through a variety of war adventures. She had been pursued by German submarines outside of Lisbon just after they had sunk a British and a Greek ship in those waters. Upon arrival at Marseilles on June 1, 1940, she was bombed as she entered port. Some of the bombs fell so close to the heavily loaded vessel that she listed about 20 degrees. Another three bombs struck so close that the force sent the stern high. The fresh-water tank holding about thirty tons was hit and its pipe broken in two, causing water to rush into the tunnel and engine room. The engine was damaged, though not so seriously as to prevent the ship from going on under her own power. During her six-day stay in Marseilles she was bombed repeatedly. From there she proceeded north of Bordeaux to Verdun, where she was again bombed several times and barely escaped magnetic mines.

On June 18, Captain Corneliussen of the *Thermopylae* and Captain Gjertsen of the *Tai Yin* were summoned by the commander of a British cruiser. Realizing the value of their cargoes, the British officer urged the ships to head for Falmouth at once, since the Germans were expected at any moment. He asked how many refugees they could take—there were thousands of them in Verdun imploring to be taken away. Hundreds of automobiles stood empty on the quay, their owners gone. Since neither of the ships had fresh water and could not get any, both had to leave without refugees. With submarines in pursuit the two ships were forced to go a hundred miles out to sea before they could cross the Channel. And contrary to orders they had to cross in the daytime in brilliant sunlight. In the Channel they passed hundreds of vessels of all kinds carrying French refugees, and Dutch tugboats towing half-finished torpedo boats and submarines to England. In British ports the *Thermopylae* was again bombed several times. On her Atlantic crossing, before arriving safely at New York, she was pursued by a German raider.

On September 9, 1940, the *Thermopylae* left Philadelphia for South Africa, where political tension was marked. Riots had broken out in the ports and a large part of the population doubted Britain's victory.

From South Africa they went to Australia. Here everything was normal and 100 per cent pro-British with absolute confidence in Britain's final victory, even though the British themselves were not altogether popular. It was only recently, when an American ship struck a mine near the coast, that the war had come close to Australia. Air patrols had failed to discover anything but a Japanese trader in the vicinity, and it was of course impossible even to whisper a suspicion that neutral freighters might have planted the mines. Rumors about German raiders filled the air; an Australian ship had sent out an emergency signal from New Zealand waters and had disappeared without a trace. Some ships had been sunk south of Freemantle.

The *Thermopylae* therefore chose to proceed east from Australia. "But we felt far away from the war and were not nervous; we only suffered from the heat," said Knudsen. "We did, however, give every ship we sighted a wide berth—it *might* be a raider, and raiders certainly inspired respect."

The ship arrived at Aden [Arabia], on New Year's Eve after a peaceful trip. The Italian radio had been busy reporting that Aden had been blown to bits, so it was a pleasant surprise to find that in more than fifty air raids only one bomb had ever hit land, and it had fallen on a rubbish heap. But since Italian Somaliland was so near that its coast could be seen from the docks, the town was prepared for an attack at any moment. Nothing however happened while the *Thermopylae* was there.

The *Thermopylae* left Aden in a convoy of twenty-five ships and proceeded to the Red Sea under an escort of no fewer than six men-of-war. She slipped out at night under cover of darkness in order to get through the Straits of Bab-el-Mandel, where it was necessary to sail right up under the Italian coast. The tension on board was terrific, but everything went well and the zigzag up the Red Sea began. The Italians had been boasting over the radio about all the ships they were sinking in these waters; in reality they had sunk only one. In Suez the *Thermopylae* waited several days for orders; the crew was not allowed ashore. Enemy planes had been over the town a number of times, but all of their bombs had fallen in the desert.

In peacetime ships pass through the Suez Canal at night, but in a blackout that is of course impossible. The *Thermopylae* left in daylight, going first to Bitter Lake and on from there the following day. Scores of vessels lay waiting to leave; the harbor at Port Said teemed with ships. Everyone was astonished to see so few soldiers in the Canal Zone.

"We had heard a good deal about the Italian danger in the Mediteranean and were therefore greatly surprised to be sent to Haifa in Palestine without escort. Haifa was full of British, Australian, and New Zealand soldiers. We brought them ammunition and mail."

The situation in Palestine didn't look good. A large part of its population speaks either German or Yiddish. To people who understand neither, these languages do not sound very different, and this fact irritates the British soldier.

In the harbor at Haifa lay the huge wreck of the ill-fated *Patria,* which had arrived in Haifa immediately after the collapse of France full of Jewish refugees. Because the poor bewildered people on board had not been able to procure a proper visa in those tragic days, the ship had been ordered to leave port. And the immigration laws of Palestine are as strict as those of the United States, if not stricter. During the night while the *Patria* still lay in dock with all her desperate refugees on board, there was a terrific explosion. The whole ship blew up, the hulk listed, and a multitude of people perished. The *Thermopylae* lay in Haifa seven months after this catastrophe, and at the end of that time dock workers and divers were still working at the ship and fishing up bodies every day. Whether survivors were allowed to remain in Palestine, Knudsen did not know, but the dead were buried in their forefathers' earth.

Airplanes had flown over Haifa several times, probably in search of the famous pipeline from Iraq, one of whose branches runs out to Haifa. But they had hit only one tank, fortunately an empty one.

The *Thermopylae* then went back to Port Said and from there to Cairo. Along the route lay enormous camps for the Italian prisoners being brought in from Libya by the thousands every day; this was just at the time when General Wavell was scoring his big triumphs. The prisoners themselves were putting barbwire around the camps and were under relatively little patrol. Cairo was in feverish activity; the town swarmed with soldiers of all nationalities and in a motley array of uniforms.

The ship received orders to load at a port on the Red Sea and return to Australia. Then suddenly a countermand to wait came. No ships were coming out of the Suez Canal, and all sorts of rumors were afloat. Neither the German nor the British radio said a word; people whispered that two ships had been sunk in the middle of the canal and that all traffic had been blocked. After an enervating layover of a week the *Thermopylae* proceeded southwards, slowly at first to Ismailia, then on to Bitter Lake. Manuevering was not easy. The wreck of a Greek ship which had struck a mine obstructed the lane. Fortunately it lay lengthwise; the canal is so narrow that had it lain crosswise, it might have stopped all traffic. German planes managed to plant mines by swooping in low over the canal and then letting them down cautiously. It required time to fish these up again. Occasionally that could not be done and they were then shot at and made to explode. If this did not succeed, it meant a further wait in the hope that something might happen. Finally it would be necessary to take a chance and let a ship pass an unexploded mine. All might go well the first time, and even the second. Perhaps it would be the fourth or the fifth ship which was blown up. Perhaps nothing would happen. The Greek ship had been split in two and many men had been killed.

At Bitter Lake about thirty vessels were waiting for orders, two of them Norwegian. In other words the canal was blocked at both the south and the north ends. German planes flew over almost every night, particularly from the south, and violent explosions and the barrage of anti-aircraft could be heard in that direction. Frequently the planes were not heard, but one could *see* the alarm. Enormous camps for Italian prisoners lay along the shore of Bitter Lake, fully illuminated to prevent anyone from escaping. If the lights went out all of a sudden, it was obvious that there were things of more important concern than stopping some prisoners from running away. The air roared with explosions all night long.

The *Thermopylae* had to wait for several weeks; she could do nothing but wait. Without a cargo on board the situation was, however, less serious for her than for several other ships carrying urgently needed war material for General Wavell's troops in Libya. Presently these began unloading cargo onto small lighters in Bitter Lake, a very primitive expedient, since there were no docks and no decent roads or any railway for further transportation. The *Thermopylae* had water and food enough on board, but not all ships were so fortunate. Ship chandlers would come from Port Said and Suez and bring them the most necessary supplies.

Slowly the difficulties began to resolve themselves. Some ships passed to the north. The *Thermopylae* was to go south. Among the first ships to pass southward was the famous aircraft carrier *Illustrious,* which had been severely damaged at Malta. It was supposed to go to Singapore for repairs, since the dry docks in Alexandria were overcrowded.

The blockade of the Suez Canal at this time was exceedingly inopportune for both the British in Libya and the Greeks, who were facing their worst ordeal. Most of the ships in the canal were Greek on their way home with war material. Report had it that the harbor of Suez was jammed with ships wanting to go north. Order and countermand followed each other in rapid succession. Finally the *Thermopylae* received orders to leave the next morning; "but in spite of our protests the pilot turned the ship northward according to orders from the British Admiralty. We understood at once that we were going to Greece."

The Suez Canal had changed greatly during these few weeks; it now swarmed with soldiers and anti-aircraft. The air was full of rumors about exploded ships and unexploded mines. But nothing happened to the *Thermopylae*.

In Alexandria there were at least two hundred naval vessels, some of them French, laid up after the armistice. French and British mariners never spoke to each other after the riots and armed encounters of the first weeks. The British cruiser *Warspite* was also there. The Norwegians knew she had taken part in the fight at Narvik and were particularly interested to hear everything about it. Norwegian and British seamen saw much of each other in this port and there was an excellent comradeship between the two; that the British held Norwegian seamen in high esteem was evident.

The *Thermopylae* loaded trucks and tanks and took on Australian troops, principally crews for the cars. The other Norwegian ships in the harbor took on the same kind of cargo and many of them finally left in the same convoy.

"We had been loading for three days," said Knudsen, "and were clear to leave on March 14. That day there was a genuine desert storm and frightful heat. It was not the first time I had experienced a sandstorm, but I've never been through anything like this one. The air was dense with a fine powder, making it impossible to see more than a few meters ahead. It penetrated everywhere in spite of closed doors and valves. There was a thick layer over tables and benches."

Finally the storm let up and late that evening the pilot came on board and took the ships out of port under a heavy sea and rain. Seven vessels, together with a strong escort of destroyers and cruisers, headed north. Hard weather raged all night long and the *Thermopylae* pitched against the wind. Sailors are not enthusiastic about tempests in peacetime, but they welcome them in wartime. Airplanes or U-boats do not operate easily in rough weather, and the higher the seas the safer the seamen feel.

"Farther north it grew colder. Sunday evening at sunset we sighted land. The next morning dawned with brilliant weather and the ships passed close to the myth-enshrined shores of Crete, which looks very much like Norway with its snow-covered mountain peaks and its fjord valleys dotted with small farmsteads and patches of green meadow. Our New Zealand friends leaned over the rail and stared toward land; after many months in the desert they probably thought it was fine to see mountains and green trees again; perhaps too it recalled their mother country, which they had not seen for more than a year. The waters between Crete and the Peloponnesus, full of islands and skerries like the rim of islands bordering the coast of Norway, sent thoughts flying homeward. The crossing was peaceful all the way and into the port of Piraeus, where we were met by Greek airplanes and torpedo chasers."

Coming to Greece was an interesting experience. Together with his comrades, the radio telegrapher went to see the Acropolis and other historical buildings in Athens. "But more than that we looked at the people in the streets, knowing how heroically they had resisted the attacks of fascist Italy and how the fascists month after month had been beaten back in spite of their superior numbers and equipment. There was hardly a young man among them. The young girls were in the service as nurses or in some other war work. The children had been evacuated. It was a city of old men and old women."

After a few days the *Thermopylae* returned to Alexandria. South of Crete the convoy was attacked by airplanes, but British and Greek planes came to their defense, and warships in the heavy escort opened a murderous fire. As soon as they were in port, the ship began loading cargo again. Everyone in Alexandria wanted news of Greece; they would hardly let us walk in peace, and not until now did we Norwegians discover how large a part of the population in Alexandria is Greek. March 25 is Greece's Independence Day and nearly all the shops in Alexandria were closed that day, since practically all its businessmen are Greeks.

On March 26 the *Thermopylae* again set out for Greece; it was an exceedingly interesting and tense trip, "although no one fully understood how tense until afterwards." Once more there were seven ships, this time escorted by four warships. Thursday the ships passed great numbers of floating mines, compelling a constant change of course. The warships were, however, extremely watchful and always discovered the mines in time to deactivate them. Machine guns shot at them until they exploded or sank.

Toward evening the *Thermopylae* suddenly received orders to follow the commodore automatically without waiting as usual for orders with every change of course. They steamed full speed ahead. At dusk, about seven o'clock, the commodore all of a sudden swung round sharply and continued full speed in the opposite direction. It looked like a peculiar maneuver, but the *Thermopylae* along with the other ships in the convoy had to stick to orders and follow. "We proceeded like that all night, full speed," said Knudsen. The maneuver caused all kinds of conjecture among officers and crew. Was it on account of floating mines? But the risk was just as great going in the opposite direction. It was difficult to find an answer to all these and a thousand other questions. Perhaps Greece had capitulated before the enormous forces attacking her. But the radio reported nothing to that effect; quite the contrary. The explanation must be looked for elsewhere. The night passed without any event of moment to the convoy and the next morning at dawn it resumed its original course northward. At sunset an Italian airplane flew in overhead; because of the dazzling sunshine no one discovered it until it was quite close. The airplane dropped a torpedo on one of the escorting destroyers but missed its target. The warships returned a violent fire, and the airplane considered it prudent not to try again. The following day the Italian radio reported a British destroyer sunk by an airplane in the identical place, demonstrating once more the unreliability of Italian broadcasts.

This time there was a noticeable nervousness in Greece; news had arrived of important concentrations of German troops on the Bulgarian-Greek frontier, and although the Greeks despised the Italians they had a deep-seated respect for the Germans. Meantime some British troops had arrived in Greece, and there was terrific activity everywhere on sea and shore.

Naval authorities now explained why the convoy had been ordered to turn back. When the convoy left Alexandria, British reconnaissance planes discovered great Italian naval units leaving their respective harbors, presumably for an attack on the British convoys bound for Greece. The British then decided to catch the Italians in a trap, using us as bait. The Italians were apparently accurately informed concerning the movements of the convoy and moved straight into its path, south of the Peloponnesus, and waited for it to turn up. "After dusk the convoy was ordered to turn back, and the British Mediterranean Fleet, which had come north from Alexandria,

continued in its place. The Italians, unfortunately for themselves, did not realize that an exchange had taken place between a relatively peaceful commercial convoy and one of
the strongest naval fleets of the world headed by *Warspite,*
an old friend of the Norwegians, the veteran from Narvik.
The British immediately opened a deadly fire and the Italians
never had a chance. The majority of the Italian ships were
sunk; the others started fleeing, panic-stricken. This was the
hardest blow yet suffered by the Italian Navy; it is called the
Battle of Matapan—Matapan being the southern promontory
of the Peloponnesus. When everything was happily over, the
British notified the convoy that the waters were clear, and
telegraphed Mussolini to "send a Red Cross ship to pick up
the Italians and Germans still swimming around." In Athens
the crew of the *Thermopylae* saw many of the prisoners from
the battle, Germans and Italians, on their way to a prison
camp.

In Piraeus people were frankly nervous about the German
troop concentrations. So far the town itself, which has a big
modern harbor with new docks and piers, had not suffered
from the war and had not yet been bombed. While the
Thermopylae was there, the next convoy from Alexandria arrived; it had been less lucky. Several of its ships had gone
down, among them two Norwegian. One of them was the M.S.
Solheim, which had been held up at Bitter Lake along with
the *Thermopylae;* only a part of her crew had been saved.
The M.S. *Perikles* had also gone down, as had a Danish ship.
Another Danish vessel, belonging to the Maersk Line, had
had her entire bridge blown off.

The return trip of the *Thermopylae* to Egypt was full of
excitement. Just south of Crete the escorting destroyers began
sinking depth bombs because U-boats had been reported in
the vicinity. The protection of the convoy was evidently too
efficient for the subs to venture an attack, and the convoy

actually never saw the submarines. "However, a squadron of airplanes did suddenly appear out of the clouds right above our masts and dropped a dozen bombs, all of which fortunately landed in the water. All ships opened a violent fire. We returned fire with our machine gun and as far as we could judge scored several hits on one attacking plane, bringing it down in a column of black smoke. But the enemy didn't give up. Three German dive bombers attacked another convoy, which we had just passed going north. Swinging into precision formation, the three swooped down upon their targets in a single line, and each hit its target. Two ships in the convoy sank: one listed and the other went right down. The third was damaged. We saw their crews get into lifeboats and row toward shore; we were right under the coast of Crete. The destroyers and a light cruiser went back to help them."

The docks in Alexandria were piled with cargo waiting to be loaded, but the *Thermopylae* got orders to wait. Two days later, on April 6, Germany declared war on Greece, and it was obvious that many plans would have to be changed. Only one convoy of five or six ships went north. After a few days two of them returned, one with her stern badly damaged; the fight must have been a hot one.

Refugees began pouring in from Greece in all kinds of vessels; with them came news of old acquaintances. One brand-new Norwegian ship, the M.S. *Bratdal*, had been sunk by an airplane near Saloniki; the crew had to row southward along the coast because the unstable conditions made it impossible to go ashore. No one knew what the risks might be. Finally after several days they were picked up by a British destroyer.

Although the Greeks had held their own valiantly against the Italians and shown indomitable courage, they were now to experience that they were up against an enemy of a different caliber. Large squadrons of German planes appeared everywhere over the blue waters of the Mediteranean, particularly around Crete, and a great many Greek ships went to the bottom. In the very port of Piraeus a Canadian munitions ship blew up from a direct hit and took eleven other ships down with it. Everything in the port—piers, docks, warehouses—which had been built up during fifteen years of a great industrial expansion was demolished. Greek officers who came over to Alexandria said that the port had been wrecked beyond use.

A Norwegian ship, the M.S. *Hav,* came in seriously damaged. A bomb had fallen a few yards in front of her bow and staved in several plates. She got orders to proceed to Singapore for repairs but never reached there; she ran into a magnetic mine in the Red Sea and was sunk.

The question of repairs was more than critical at the time. Wrecked or half-wrecked ships were floating everywhere. To get repairs at Malta was out of the question since the island was under almost constant bombardment; Haifa did not have docks large enough; and the port of Alexandria was desperately overcrowded. Every day more crippled ships came limping in to port, requiring expert assistance. All ships which could somehow manage on their own went to Singapore with its famous dry docks.

So the *Thermopylae* did not go back to Greece; it was to know Greece's tragedy at a distance. "On the contrary we were presently ordered to undertake another hazardous crossing, namely to try to run the blockade at Malta. Conditions there were known to be critical. Vital supplies were depleted. One convoy after another had attempted to break through, only to be forced to turn back. Now it was the *Thermopylae's* turn to try."

The convoy consisted of six vessels. Four of them were Norwegian Wilhelmsen Line ships—the *Talabot* and *Thermopylae,* and the tankers *Svenö* and *Höegh Hood.* The others were the Danish ship *Amerika* and the British cargo ship *Settler,* the latter with a colored crew and white officers. "It is undeniable that we felt like a suicide squad when we left Alexandria, though we probably had the strongest escort that a single convoy ever had. The greater part of the British Mediterranean Fleet accompanied us. Being slower than the others, the two tankers led. Then our two freighters from the Wilhelmsen Line together with the Danish and the British ships, protected by four cruisers and two destroyers. The morning we left port, May 6, 1941, we saw many other ships leaving the harbor. They kept their distance, but it was comforting to know about them.

"This trip to Malta was hard on the nerves of most of us. Chances of getting through safely appeared to be less than fifty-fifty. Sleep was almost unknown. The first two days were idyllic enough; it was not until the third day that enemy planes appeared on the horizon. The escort was, however, too powerful for them. An aircraft carrier in the vicinity virtually spewed out chaser planes which charged at them, and we were protected by a terrific barrage of anti-aircraft fire. The enemy planes had to give up and dropped their bombs into the sea in order to get away faster; we saw enormous columns of water leap skyward.

"Planes were not the only danger. Floating mines drifted everywhere, the escort shooting constantly until the mines either sank or exploded. And our escort was so expert at it that no ship struck a mine.

"Toward evening while the convoy was approaching Malta, we saw something which we didn't like: one by one the warships swung round and turned back into the night—which is to say that we were left almost alone through the most perilous waters of the trip. Only two small destroyers went with us the whole way.

"The next morning we lay right outside of Valletta, the

capital of Malta. A signal was flashed from land: 'The channel is not clear. Wait!' Then orders came to proceed inward one ship at a time in the wake of a mine sweeper. The *Thermopylae* crept slowly through the narrow entrance without a pilot. The channel was narrow enough as it was, but to make it even worse a ship which had been sunk in the middle of it made proper steering still more difficult. Throngs of people on the docks and piers hailed our arrival—cheering, clapping their hands: we were the first convoy to get through in more than three months.

"Visible evidence of the fearful work of bombers began to appear along the course as the tug towed us in toward the anchoring place. We had no sooner thrown out cables forward and aft than air-raid sirens set up an alarm. 'Get to the shelter,' they shouted from land. The *Thermopylae* didn't even have her gangplank out, so the crew slithered down the ship's side on a rope ladder. Some fell into the water, of course, but did manage to get themselves out again. The shelter had been cut right into the mountainside and we went in. A curious, monotonous sound rose from the floor; as soon as our eyes had adjusted themselves to the dim light, they could see black-clad women in a kind of national costume kneeling in prayer and running the beads of their rosaries through their fingers. It made us uncomfortable to be in there, so we went out again to look at the planes. Neither of the two tankers had come into port. A mine exploded right in front of the bow of the *Amerika* but did no damage.

"The *Thermopylae* had come alongside at 10:30 A.M., just as the first air-raid alarm sounded. At 12:10 P.M. there was a second alarm, at 2:45 P.M. a third. It was all a part of the day's routine and what we men had to get accustomed to during our three months in the harbor; and what the Maltese had had to endure for a couple of years.

"Though our trip to Malta had been dangerous, our reward was great. We were treated with matchless kindness. The Maltese did everything to show their gratitude; concerned themselves to the utmost to protect our lives. Each ship was assigned her own shelter; and they were good shelters, hewn deep into the soft, yellow tuff cliffs. Every man had a camp cot himself, so the men were well cared for when they had to spend the night there. Many of the inhabitants of the islands slept in shelters every night; they had become cave dwellers again. The town above our heads, Valletta, had fared badly. Part of it had been leveled, and nowhere was there a single street without ruined buildings and empty, grinning façades.

"Malta is a fascinating and colorful island, a yellow block of tuff rising from the sea. The stone is soft and easily cut; there are interesting prehistoric underground temples hewn deep into it. The quality of the stone, its softness and smoothness, is the principal reason why so few Maltese, relatively speaking, have been killed during the war; they can live quite comfortably as cave dwellers. Valletta has a number of beautiful old palaces, though several of the most characteristic have been destroyed. There are still many houses of the true Maltese type with second-story balconies from which the women of the household can observe street life without themselves being seen. It's a type brought to Malta from Rhodes by the Maltese knights.

"The Maltese language is a curious mixture of Arabian and Latin (perhaps more Catalan than anything else) together with several other Mediterranean tongues; it has, for example, retained many Greek words. Nothing will infuriate a Maltese more than being called an Italian. The fascists exploited Malta to the limit in their propaganda about a greater Italy, including it as a matter of course on all maps of the future Roman Empire. But the population itself would have nothing to do with the Italians and the events of the war have not made them more tolerant. Meantime it is generally asserted that the clergy are on the side of Italy and that they have sent enormous sums of money to Rome. At present the only valid currency is some notes printed on only one side and circulating exclusively on Malta.

"Events of the last few years have united the Maltese and filled them with a fervent patriotism. Their island was the most bombed spot on earth. Yet there was never any sign of panic among them; on the contrary, many had become so reckless through their exposure to constant danger that they did not bother to go into the shelters. The first days we were there," said Knudsen, "the aerial attack was practically uninterrupted, but after the end of the battle of Crete things quieted down a little and we had only three or four alarms during the day and about as many at night. Sometimes people were killed right at the entrance to a shelter; they were so interested in seeing what was happening that they forgot to look out for their safety. The worst thing which we saw happened to a dock worker we knew: he lost his wife and all of his eight children one night when they had decided to sleep in town for a change."

After the unloading the ship lay waiting for orders. The port itself was in very bad shape. The worst catastrophe had occurred when a destroyer struck a mine in the main part of the harbor: her whole crew was killed. One navy wharf was demolished and a floating dock sunk. Of five dry docks three were wholly destroyed and two badly damaged. The power plant was demolished, though it didn't matter much since another one had been built in the mountainside. When the convoy arrived, there was only one freighter in port, namely the *Essex;* but airplanes came daily on routine flights between Gibraltar and Alexandria. Aside from the port, the airdrome was a principal target for the bombers. German planes were considered far more dangerous than Italian, which usually dropped their bombs into the sea and hurried away. The anti-aircraft performed brilliantly, and the whole island was a barbwire network of fortifications.

"The situation when we were there was in many ways an exceedingly tough one for the population," said Knudsen. "The air-borne invasion of Crete had naturally created nervousness and many feared that the same thing might happen here. Added to this was the fact that the wives and children of many officers and crew members of the British Mediterranean Fleet were quartered there, and they were in constant fear about the fate of their loved ones. Death messages poured in every day, shaking the little community to its foundations; loss of life was at a terribly high rate in Crete. At one time it was decided to move some of the most irreplaceable machines and about three thousand workers to Alexandria; and we were already engaged in loading, when a countermand came. Alexandria had been so violently bombed that it scarcely seemed a less hazardous haven than Malta."

To the Norwegians the stay in Malta was a wonderful experience, even though the long layup frayed their nerves. The Maltese never tired of demonstrating their gratitude and affection. They arranged excursions everywhere on the island; took them to the grotto where Paul was shipwrecked on his voyage to Rome; kept constantly inviting them to their homes. "Many of the Maltese had no idea where Norway was, though you may be sure they knew before we left. We enjoyed almost frightening popularity; some of the boys even married Maltese girls."

A tragic thing happened to the Norwegians during their stay. Captain Bjarne Kristiansen of the M.S. *Talabot* died of sunstroke while he was out bathing with Captain Corneliussen. Practically the whole population of the island came to the funeral; there were representatives of the Army and the Navy there, as well as of the local authorities, "so we could plainly see how great their sympathy for us was."

Finally, after an interminable wait the *Thermopylae* got orders to load with scrap iron. "We left July 23, carrying some passengers, a crew to man the guns, and a supply of explosives, with everything in readiness for sinking the ship immediately if necessary. A couple of destroyers accompanied us out and it appeared that we could rely on the protection of the British Navy and the RAF. As it happened we didn't see a single ship. We left early one morning and at sunset the same day passed the strongly fortified Italian island of Pantelleria in the narrowest part of the strait between Sicily and Tunisia. The ships traveled in pairs at top speed. An enormous light spread across the sky as we passed the island and the wireless flashed out demanding to know who we were. The ships gave no answer, just kept on sailing as close as possible to the North African coast. It was pitch dark, and we were fearful of mines. Nobody slept; everyone wore a life belt, and it could not be denied that some were pretty nervous. All was clear to send out an SOS.

"The following forenoon our convoy was attacked by three bombers arriving from different directions. The ships were two cable lengths apart and traveled in a constant zigzag. A torpedo came straight at the *Amerika*. The captain, seeing it in time, shifted the course sharply to port, and the torpedo missed the propeller by a few feet, while the other torpedoes went far wide of their targets. The planes came back and began machine-gunning; the *Amerika* had two four-and-a-half-inch wires shot to pieces and a man wounded in the shoulder. The sea looked as if a hailstorm had struck it. The *Thermopylae* escaped damage. Fifteen minutes later, when the ships had got back into formation, four big bombers flew in at a height of about 6,000 feet. When they were directly above us, all four discharged their bombs at the same instant. We saw them in the air and several fell not very far away, but there were no hits.

"We sent out SOS signals. A few hours later the ships in the lead unit called for help; they had been attacked by torpedo planes. Then, a very little later, unit three sent out the same signals. The following day unit three, again attacked by torpedo planes, called for help; this time the *Hoegh Hood* was hit in tank number one, port side. The ship was, however, able to proceed at a speed of ten knots and did arrive safely. The hole in her side was almost large enough to admit a rowboat.

"We arrived at Gibraltar July 26. There were many ships there, among them a number of Norwegian ones. The tankers arrived the following day, one of them with a big hole in the side. The tension now being released, we began to look ahead —where were we to go? We seemed somehow to have the feeling that we had had enough of war for a while.

"All was calm in Gibraltar: no alarm, no demolished houses. Truly idyllic after Malta. One day the crew of a torpedoed Norwegian ship which had been in a convoy arrived. A third of the ships in that convoy had gone down, showing how singularly fortunate the *Thermopylae* had been. The *Thermopylae* left Gibraltar in a convoy of four. Feeling safe after a couple of days, we left the convoy and traveled alone full speed to New York, arriving there without further adventures."

The radio telegrapher, Knudsen, who told the greater part of the story of the *Thermopylae*, finally reached the goal of his greatest desire, namely, the Royal Norwegian Air Force in Toronto. There he worked as a radio specialist, and later went to England with the Air Force. Captain Corneliussen received the War Medal and St. Olav's Medal in recognition of his excellent conduct of the ship.

In 1942 the *Thermopylae* was sunk in the Mediterranean in a second attempt to reach Malta.

II

The Norwegian merchant marine had many women in its service when the war broke out. Just how many is not known, but it is safe to say at least two hundred were employed as stewardesses and waitresses, especially on passenger ships. Though as a matter of principle the general view has been that a more proper place for women to work would be on shore, there have nevertheless been obstacles in the way of immigration legislation, as well as other difficulties, so that even now a few women continue to be found in the service. Many have preferred to sail as long as they can because they like being on ships. And, said Helga Aabel, now Mrs. Rönsen and in the employ of Nortraship, "It's the only way for poor people to see anything of the world."

These women have been through the same dangers as their men comrades. The story of Helga Aabel is typical. On April 7, 1940, she was on the S.S. *Bergensfjord* as a stewardess in the engineers' mess hall when the ship left Bergen. Helga was delighted to be employed on a beautiful modern ship. At the time the large number of German ships riding in the harbor entrance as they passed through did not escape notice. The news of the invasion of their country on the ninth was too awful to describe, she says.

After a few months in the States, she went out again, this time on a sunshine cruise to South America—Buenos Aires and Rio—with sightseeing trips everywhere. There the

Thermopylae came into port after her perilous adventures in the Mediterranean, and was now by way of reward being sent on a quiet trip to Australia via the Panama Canal. Helga did not like the thought of a protracted stay in South America. What with a nephew, Rolf Jensen, and two women on board the *Thermopylae*, Helga decided to see more of the world and signed on the ship. At Sydney a change of orders came: they were to go to Egypt. This didn't sound like a sunshine trip, but neither did she want to sign off in Australia. After a quiet voyage they reached Alexandria, where all was rather peaceful. There had been only one air raid during their three weeks there.

At Alexandria the *Thermopylae* got orders to proceed to Malta with ammunition. She crossed the Mediterranean in convoy but as an old ship found it difficult to keep up with the more modern ships. There had been several air attacks, but Helga brushed these off with, "Shucks, they were only Italian planes that were afraid to come down and dropped their bombs from way up. They never hit a thing." On the third day, less than twenty-four hours off Malta, something went wrong with the steering gear, and the *Thermopylae*, unable to continue zigzagging, was ordered to turn back—a long way to go. Four destroyers escorted her.

At 10:00 A.M., January 2, 1942, it happened. Helga had just finished her work in the officers' mess hall, when the shooting began. She opened the door and saw a fiery red bomb come whirling down. After that she had only some confused memories of a lifeboat. She was trying to run away; three men were holding her down. She saw the third engineer; his face was black; he was waving his hands. The poor man had been badly burned. She blacked out again. When she woke up, she was in a ship's cabin, this time on a British destroyer. Someone was bending over her putting stitches in her head. This lasted only a moment. The smell of ether blotted out everything. The next time she woke up she found herself in a hospital in Alexandria.

A German bomber had dived straight down on the *Thermopylae* and had struck the deck directly outside the officers' mess, throwing Helga thirty feet along the deck. She lay unconscious, her head and leg badly wounded. The captain found her and carried her into a lifeboat. The second engineer lying unconscious a few yards away was also carried into the lifeboat, by the first engineer. Three men of the crew of nearly forty men were killed. The *Thermopylae* didn't go down but had to be sunk by two torpedoes.

Then came a long, dull time in an Alexandria hospital for Helga Aabel. Her condition was critical. A splinter had entered her head less than a millimeter from the optical nerve. Her leg had been all but blown off. She was delirious, couldn't sleep, was always seeing the fiery bomb the instant it struck the deck. The days were unnerving with their continued air raids and news of the Germans' rapid advance through Libya.

Finally, however, skilled surgery, excellent care, and a healthy constitution pulled her through. After three and a half months she was allowed to leave the hospital, fortunately on her own ship the *Bergensfjord,* now a troopship bound for Cape Town. Among those on board were the skipper of the *Thermopylae;* also Mrs. Elna Kristensen, who had been a stewardess on the *Thermopylae* for several years; and a doctor, so that Helga could get the medical care she urgently needed. She was still hardly able to walk. The *Bergensfjord* was also carrying more than a thousand German prisoners, all of whom sang and seemed happy to be out of the hell of war.

At Cape Town there was a further delay of a month. Meantime Helga was slowly gaining control of the wounded leg, and boarded a Norwegian ship, the *Nordahl,* en route to the United States. There was a stop at Bahia for coal; so far all was well. When they were less than twenty-four hours off

New York, a new calamity struck. Helga was in the captain's
cabin typing. A violent explosion sent wood fragments flying
through the air; the whole ship creaked. Helga made for the
lifeboat as fast as she could. She had her safety vest on. The
torpedo had hit the cargo, which is what saved those midships.
Everyone reached the lifeboat and was saved. One man fell
into the sea but was picked up by a destroyer, and arrived in
New York ahead of the others. Those in the lifeboat rowed
around for a while and saw two other ships of the convoy
sunk by a U-boat, one of them a tanker hit by a gigantic fireball exploding against her engine.

Helga Aabel cannot go to sea again. She finishes off her
story by telling that the nephew, Rolf Jensen, was with
Thermopylae went she went down. At Alexandria he had
signed on a British hospital ship and he had gone with her
to Tobruk shortly after the Germans were driven back from
there. The hospital ship was torpedoed by the Germans. This
experience was different. When the *Thermopylae* was bombed,
he had managed to keep completely calm, had gone down into
the cabin and succeeded in rescuing documents and money—
had even taken time to change his clothes. But carrying
wounded men on board under constant air attacks, he wrote
to her, was worse than anything he had ever known.

North Africa

~~~~~~

23

Norwegian Sailors Interned

The morning after I arrived in Algiers, I got in touch with the captain and crew of the *Bosporus* of the Mediterranean Line. The ship had been in Marseilles; immediately before the armistice she had received orders from the Norwegian consulate to proceed to some Allied or neutral harbor. She had been on her way to Gibraltar but had not dared go into a Spanish harbor since under the circumstances no one knew whether Franco's Spain could be considered very neutral. So, for reasons which are not altogether clear, the *Borporus* had chosen to go to Algiers.

Almost three weeks after the armistice between Germany and France, North Africa had not yet made up its mind. No one knew what to believe or how to act. Its people realized of course that France had suffered the greatest defeat in her millennial history, but they had not *seen* with their eyes the desperate humiliation of the whole thing as the French at home had. And here in Algiers, "the granary of the Roman Empire," there was no lack of anything yet; there had been enough of food and all other necessities of life. But events in Oran, which is the second largest port in Algiers, had made a profound impression. The English feared—and not without reason—that the French Mediterranean Fleet would be delivered to the Germans. They therefore went to Oran's naval

base, Mers-el-Kebir, and made the following proposals to the
French Fleet anchored there: it could join the British Fleet
or go under British escort to some French port in the Western
Hemisphere—Martinique, for instance—and remain inactive
for the duration. If it chose to do neither, the British would
shoot. Either under pressure from Germany or through lack
of will or through collaborators in Vichy, the French chose
to fight and lost many important ships. Vichy and Germany
on the other hand, gained far more than they lost in those
more or less damaged units of the Navy: for Vichy succeeded
in utilizing the episode as propaganda to poison the minds of
Frenchmen and North Africans against the British. Neither
radio nor newspapers even mentioned the second alternative,
namely the offer to send the Fleet under safe escort to the
Western Hemisphere—an offer which could hardly have hurt
even the most tender sensibilities. Nine hundred and ninety-
nine out of a thousand Frenchmen still ignore this simple fact
and the enormous bitterness against England derives partly
from this episode, or rather from the censors' neat way of
utilizing it. These tactics in communicating "news" went on
for three years and explain a good deal.

Everyone in Algiers was hostile toward the British, but
beyond that the attitude was uncertain. Vichy did whatever
it could to influence minds in the direction it wanted. It knew
the old method of *panem et circenses*. As the bread supply
grew shorter the number and coloring of the plays and parades
grew more spectacular. Most of these performances had a
military character and were well calculated to please the color
loving natives. In the month of July, Algiers welcomed a new
governor, Admiral Abrial, "the hero of Dunkirk." In white
uniform resplendent with decorations he drove up from the
harbor in an elegant limousine surrounded by the Foreign
Legion and native troops on sleek black or white horses. It
was a beautiful sight and undoubtedly contributed much

oward heightening morale. It was well known that Admiral
Abrial had been the last Frenchman to leave Dunkirk and
that his valiant last-minute fight had saved many French
troops. What was not known in Algiers at the time is that
from Dunkirk the Admiral had proceeded to Cherbourg and
there surrendered all the present units of the French Navy to
the Germans without putting up any fight at all. Nor was it
known that he had been a German prisoner of war for about
a week in the famous Castle Königstein in Saxony. It was here
that General Ruge of Norway was imprisoned because of his
refusal to give his word of honor not to fight the Germans,
and it was from here that General Giraud dramatically escaped. The way out was easy for Admiral Abrial: he, together
with about one fifth of the French generals and admirals, was
given his freedom, with the thanks and compliments of the
Nazis. That is why Vichy thought he would have such an
elevating effect on the morale of Algiers. And the population
of North Africa continued to ignore the painful facts.

In this rather tense atmosphere the crew of the Norwegian
ship *Bosporus* were roaming around with little to do. Their
forced idleness had now lasted a few weeks, and they were
still busy putting their ship in readiness, scraping off the rust
and repainting her everywhere. The skipper kept wiring the
Norwegian Government and the Shipping Director in London
continually, and he was told to leave. But that was not easily
done, with small torpedo boats guarding the harbor entrance
and a gigantic net against submarines stretched from pier to
pier. Every day it became increasingly evident that the French
had no intention of releasing their prey.

Although the weather was fine, the boys had a rotten
time of it. They were always discussing the possibilities of
escape, though these appeared less than small. Gibraltar, the
nearest Allied port except Malta, lay more than five hundred
miles away. And Malta could be reached only through fascist-

infested waters. They speculated about the outcome of the war and what might be expected. As long as the Norwegians could live aboard their own comfortable ship and get paid a small part of their wages, they felt comparatively well off. But they could not help seeing, practically every day, the transports full of prisoners on their way to the gigantic concentration and labor camps in the interior. The Germans were promoting with all their might the building of a railway to the south (the frequently mentioned missing link between the Mediterranean countries and Equatorial Africa), along with an important branch line to Dakar. That would mean a line of strategic importance once the offensive against South America and the Western Hemisphere was ready to begin, a likelihood now supposedly not far away. The project counted on building the line with slave labor, and thousands of prisoners from French concentration camps were being brought overseas to work in desert sand and heat. The work had been started years ago by a French administration, but had proved too hard for the native Arabs and Berbers. The Nazi superrace, however, was never too scrupulous about sacrificing human lives; on the contrary, the more anti-fascist enemies it could rid the world of the better. All kinds of people arrived for this labor: Spaniards, Austrians, German anti-Nazis, Czechs, Poles. Many had fought on the side of the French in this unhappy war. And to the harbor of Algiers came very gruesome reports concerning working conditions in the Sahara. Were the Norwegians to risk that kind of fate?

After six weeks in Algiers, I succeeded in obtaining a visa for Morocco, and all the Norwegian sailors envied me the prospect of getting out to the Atlantic, which from the point of view of the Mediterranean seemed to offer unlimited possibilities.

Casablanca was wonderful. It is a modern, newly built town with magnificent and audacious architecture. The vast horizon of the Atlantic, pregnant with promises for the future, spreads before it. I went down to the harbor hoping to find Norwegian ships, but the harbor was not accessible to the general public. Negro soldiers with guns and obviously belligerent intentions guarded all entrances to the port proper. I saw the famous harbor only once, and that was on the day seven months later when I finally left the city.

But it was not hard to find Norwegians; for there were no fewer than ten Norwegian ships in port. The crews lived on board and were allowed ashore at certain hours. In every restaurant and bar one heard Norwegian spoken without any restrictions; sailors aired their opinions about Casablanca, Frenchmen, Negroes and Arabs, confident that nobody understood a word of their exceedingly free talk.

Casablanca is now world-famous and possesses an interest which it hardly had in 1940. It is a rather fantastic city. As late as 1915 it was only a small native village, dirty, not even "picturesque," with exactly one European house outside its walls. Now the population is rapidly approaching 200,000; the town is beautiful and spacious; all the main thoroughfares are built with arcades for protection against rain and sun; there are large parks, avenues of waving palms, and the world's largest outdoor swimming pool, which is built in the rocks close to the Atlantic and open all year round. Morocco has a far more progressive social system than France herself. During the last twenty-five years the country has passed through a rapid development, and it is one of the few countries in the world which did not experience any kind of crisis during that period. The city and the country around it have expanded at a furious rate, and there is a kind of free and generous air about the city itself and its colorful population.

Morocco was much less under the influence of Vichy than Algiers: it had a more independent status, was farther away from the menace and the hypnotizing or paralyzing influence

of the Germans. An enormous "underground railroad" passe
through the country; French pilots, Central European Social
ists, and escaped British war prisoners came to the countr
and were somehow smuggled into Gibraltar or some othe
Allied or neutral territory. No one knew exactly how; no on
could rely on his neighbor, no one dared express his hones
opinion. Here were still traces of a free press; the courageou
little newspaper *La Presse Marocaine* was repeatedly retire
from circulation for shorter or longer periods because of it
too openly demonstrated sympathies with the Allies or it
frank praise of General de Gaulle. It could not write ver
much without running up against an interdict. "France wa
originally called *Gaul*," it wrote truthfully and innocently. I
French, however, the word *Gaul* ought to be spelled *Gaule*
through a "misprint" it was spelled *Gaulle*. This escaped th
censor. And all Casablanca smiled for half a day until thi
high treason was discovered in the proper quarters and th
newspaper was promptly suppressed for another fortnight.

The Norwegians hated being stuck in Casa. Why ha
they ever conceived the unhappy idea of looking to Nort
Africa for escape during those confused days of the armistice
Well, because they had believed that France would continu
the struggle from the colonies; Premier Reynaud had mo:
emphatically said so. But old Marshal Pétain succeede
Reynaud. Three ships did manage to get out of the harbc
before a blockade was effected, but after a few days the sam
iron custody was enforced here as in Algiers. It grew steadil
worse; the French took away parts of the engines, with muc
more dangerous consequences than in the comparatively quie
port of Algiers; here the crippled ships were exposed to th
fury of autumn storms from the Atlantic without any natur;
protection and were unable to maneuver in the harbor. The
the ships drifted between enormous piers, damaging severa
harbor constructions, and the French realized that somethin

different would have to be done with them. Before long four
or five were given orders to go north to Port-Lyautey. Soon
afterwards I went up there to see how the Norwegians were.

The ships had been placed in the meandering outlet of
the river Oued-Sebou, several miles in from the ocean. It is
a flat, dull country; along the river is a marsh, and to get to
firm ground the men had to cross a sort of primitive plank
bridge. A hundred yards away you could see no river whatever, so the sight of twenty or thirty ships in what appeared
to be the middle of the marsh was certainly a surprising one.
There were Danish, Polish, and Greek ships, all interned for
the duration.

The nearest town, Port-Lyautey, was about a two-hour
walk away and offered few attractions—only one small thea-
ter and some rather bad restaurants. The men were not allowed to stay in the hotels overnight because the space was
needed for Frenchmen, who claimed priority.

The morale of the Norwegian seamen was low. None of
them could speak a word of French or Spanish, to say nothing
of Arabic. Occasionally letters would come from Norway by
way of the United States, after a trip of several months. Norwegian newspapers did not exist; once or twice the seamen's
union paper arrived. No one had any idea what had happened
in Norway during the war, which towns had been burnt, and
so on. They were forbidden to listen to Norwegian short-wave
broadcasts from London and Boston, but of course everybody
did anyway. These were, however, insufficient and irregular,
and didn't always come through, partly because of the surveillance of the Vichy French. It took a long time after one
had left Morocco before he found out what had actually been
happening in the world; in spite of a certain liberty of movement, the Norwegians were in a gigantic concentration camp
mentally and spiritually.

Three other Norwegian ships were transferred from the

danger zone of Casablanca to the smaller port of Safi, farther to the south. It was better than Port-Lyautey, though not by much. Language instruction was started in a few places but only on private initiative and without any official backing. The men were left pretty much to themselves and their gloomy thoughts. Some of them could take it; others became despondent; and at least one of them committed suicide.

It is true that the morale of the sailors was not good. But perhaps it was this very fact that stimulated them to action. Those first to escape from Casablanca were six men from the M.S. *Gran;* they set out in motorboats and made directly for Gibraltar. Their safe arrival was confirmed in a telegram from London, and this in turn put new courage and enterprise into the whole lot. Week after week, month after month, we learned about new attempts at escape. Since Port-Lyautey lay a hundred miles north of Casa and only about a hundred miles from Gibraltar, it was natural that most of the boats should go out from here. It is possible that the French guards shut their eyes and did not watch the outlet of the river too closely on dark nights. They threatened to shoot but never did. A certain school for French cadets in Port-Lyautey read General de Gaulle's pamphlets with eagerness. Several times French pilots or sailors were also known to have tried to reach Gibraltar. Some of the Norwegian lifeboats were caught on their way out of port, but the punishment was not too severe —usually only a few days' or weeks' imprisonment in a comparatively idyllic prison. One sailor, named Horten, was captured four times before he succeeded in escaping. Some of the men went to Spain or to Spanish Morocco by mistake and they generally had to spend a few weeks or months there before they were sent on to Gibraltar; their opinion of Spanish prisons, particularly those in Morocco, is far from flattering.

It seems that all of the Norwegians arrived safely after the hurricane of February, 1941, which struck Portugal with particular fury but hardly touched the coast of Morocco. A Norwegian boat had ventured out just a few days before, and for a long time there was serious apprehension that the men had been overcome by the storm. As a matter of fact, however, the boat arrived safely. The unknown drowned may have been part of a Danish crew said to have disappeared at the time. It must not be forgotten that the Casablancans, with their lifelong experience of the dangerous coastal waters and tides and of the awful sucking surf of the fiercely pounding Atlantic, believed any attempt at escape in a lifeboat tantamount to suicide, and that they therefore were skeptical of the reports that the boats arrived safely.

All the captains received offers to sail under the French flag, and all of them refused. A Danish captain in Dakar, however, accepted the offer and then somehow managed to delude his French escort and steam right into Gibraltar. Exulting letters came to us from friends aboard his ship: "Finally we are on the right side! Now we shall be able to fight!"

In February, 1941, the French authorities requisitioned the tanker *Jaspis,* the one and only Norwegian vessel in Casablanca harbor at the time. The crew were given one hour's notice and had to abandon ship practically empty-handed. Many lost most of their personal belongings. And along with the ship went also an excellent Norwegian library. The harbor was already full of French ships laid up by the drastic terms of the armistice. The crew of the *Jaspis* were placed in various hotels, but the French seemed not to know what to do with these guests. Another Norwegian crew followed immediately, this one from the M.S. *Gabon,* which had been in Dakar and had likewise been requisitioned. They told about life and conditions there, where there were eight Norwegian ships; everything in Dakar from climate to restrictions had been much more intolerable than in Casablanca.

We were particularly interested to hear about the unfortunate attack of the British and Gaullist navies on Dakar in September of 1940. Here, too, as in Algiers and Casablanca, the Norwegian ships found themselves in an unenviable position in the harbor, incapable of maneuvering under the rain of bombs because of the removal of essential parts of their engines. Everyone, Norwegians as well as Frenchmen, hoped and prayed that the British would win, for up to that time Vichy had gained very little sympathy in Dakar. It was generally asserted that Dakar wanted to surrender immediately but that a telegram came from Vichy warning that the Germans threatened reprisals against the two million French prisoners in Germany if the town did not try to defend itself. The resistance was not strong and hardly serious. "If the British had held on for another hour, Dakar would have surrendered," said the men, bitterly disappointed; it was horrible to see the British Navy take off again, leaving nothing but ruins and an enormous loss of prestige. The Danish M.S. *Tacoma,* which lay anchored in among the Norwegian ships, was hit and five men were killed; the fire lasted for days and seriously threatened the other ships. The Norwegian consulate in Dakar was also hit.

The crews from the *Jaspis* and the *Gabon* felt uneasy about the future; they thought that Vichy was looking for some way to stop them from mischief. The air was thick with rumors about concentration camps. Then something entirely unexpected happened. With the lack of logic which always characterized Vichy and which showed how unstable and divergent both individual and political views there were, the crews of both vessels, sixty-two men in all, were allowed to proceed to Portugal. It seemed incredible, and until their very last moment in the harbor the men, in breathless tension, expected to be taken off the ship and thrown into a concentration camp. But they left all right. I happened to leave on the same ship, the Portuguese steamer *Nyassa,* since I had finally succeeded in obtaining my America visa. For the men this was a wonderful voyage back to freedom and a chance to fight. Practically all of them went to England and are now sailing in either the Norwegian Navy or merchant marine. In June, 1941, three months after our departure, the French took over all the Norwegian ships in Morocco and put the crews in concentration camps.

24

Escape

It was in Algiers during the summer of 1940 that I first met Sverre. He was then first mate on the beautiful motor ship *Bosporus* interned there by the French. What a beautiful ship she was in her clear, bright colors and bold modern lines! My mind is still stamped with the memory of her and the picturesque harbor in which she lay—the grayish-green cactus on yellow cliffs, the mountain slopes with white Arab houses offset by clusters of red tomatoes on their walls, and the greenish-blue, glittering Mediterranean filling the whole horizon.

The Norwegian and Danish sailors in port were always talking about escaping to Malta or Gibraltar, but their situation looked pretty hopeless. The mouth of the harbor is a narrow passage between closely guarded breakwaters. In addition the passage itself had been closed by a net stretched between the moles as a protection against attacking U-boats and as a safeguard against any ship's escaping "for the duration."

When I got my visa in 1941 and left Algiers after about a year's forced stay, I felt sorry for the men doomed to rot away in the backwater of the Vichy regime, risking concentration camps and arbitrary treatment at any time.

More than a year and a half had passed when upon returning to my hotel in Brooklyn one night in the spring of 1942, I found the following note waiting for me: "Greetings from Algiers and Casablanca." The signature *Bosporus* could

clearly mean only one thing: Sverre! Though his ship was due
to leave New York that day, I saw him for about a half hour
in a restaurant not far from the dock, and he told me his story.

It had looked hopeless, he confessed. As for himself, he
spent one year and five days in the port of Algiers, and that
was plenty. He was the first man to escape. One dark night,
July 1, 1941, he and some companions decided to make a try.
The French had long before removed the lifeboats from the
Bosporus in order to prevent the crew from escaping, but
Sverre and his shipmates stole a boat somewhere, perhaps not
wholly without the consent of the robbed party. It began to
rain as the boat slipped slowly out into the dark night. Two
men had to get out of the boat and hold the obstruction net
down with their feet while the others stared up at the moles
where the guards were just being changed. Sharp orders
echoed through the soft rain. They got across the net. Beyond
it silence. Not a word was spoken. They rowed northward,
past all the places they knew so well, the beach, the shacks.
After a few hours they dared to hoist sail. At dawn they
could not see land any more. They then set their course
straight west to Gibraltar. The worst "danger" threatened
from a big passenger liner they met near the heights of Oran;
she all but sailed into their tiny craft and afterwards insisted
on saving the boys, which was understandable enough since
they most certainly must have looked shipwrecked. But they
innocently went on fishing and signaled back that all was well.

With sail and oars it took them ten days to get to Gibraltar. They had no engine of any kind. As the crow flies, the
distance would be somewhat more than five hundred miles:
with the detours they had to take in order to avoid danger
zones it probably got to be nearer six hundred. Provisions for
the six of them consisted of sixty-five liters of water and seventeen loaves of bread.

The boat sailed right into the harbor of Gibraltar with

a small Norwegian flag flying merrily in the breeze and probably causing a little sensation. Said Sverre: "We brought a lot of valuable information from Algiers about the Germans and Italians there. A German commission had come on board the *Bosporus* several times; and there were a number of interesting things to note in and about the harbor." The British showed much friendliness and a great eagerness to listen; among other things Sverre had with him was a copy of the logbook of the *Bosporus,* which contained a mass of details from their stay in Algiers.

At the request of the British, Sverre stayed in Gibraltar for three months to help receive Norwegians who began pouring into the harbor from everywhere. "Hardly a day passed without arrivals—in motorboats, fishing boats, small rowboats, on rafts." One man had fallen overboard and actually came in swimming. They came from Marseilles, from Oran and Algiers, from Casablanca and Port-Lyautey and Safi in Morocco. In Algiers a reward was offered for the capture of Sverre and his shipmates, but the companions they left behind got blood in their eyes from their comrades' example and one boatload of men after the other disappeared from the *Bosporus.* "The mate should show the way," said Sverre. His was the only boat which managed to sail all the way to Gibraltar; the others landed somewhere in Spain and the men were sent on by land.

Sverre paid particular tribute to the men who escaped from the *President Herren-Schmidt* in Marseilles. The largest city in the then "non-occupied zone" of France was full of anti-Nazi elements and of people scared to death of the day when the Germans would be occupying all of France. On the other hand, German soldiers and willing Vichy satellites kept a close guard over the harbor, anxious that no one should escape. An airplane was sent in search of the fleeing lifeboat but fortunately did not spot it.

Other Norwegians in Marseilles lost courage and thought

escape hopeless. One boy signed on a German ship after an enervating wait of almost a year. This pleased the Germans, since it appeared that finally one of these Norwegians was showing reasonableness and would fall in line with the master race. Their joy didn't last long, however, for the boy ran away in Valencia, was sent to Gibraltar and there joined the free Norwegian fleet.

After a few months Sverre got tired of Gibraltar and went to the British Admiralty to explain that he had really run away from Algiers in order to go out sailing and that he had been laid up for a longer time than he liked. The British were sympathetic. They had a small French ship in port which they had seized a few weeks earlier. Could Sverre and his friends take it to England? Certainly they could! Sverre made up a crew of thirty-six Norwegian seamen, all escapees from French and North African ports and all wanting to go out again. In lieu of the proper staff of officers, Sverre made a machinist function as chief engineer and made several other rather irregular assignments. He showed me the permission which the British Admiralty had given him to take the ship to England; he hadn't got his Master's papers yet. He also showed me another document from the Admiralty conveying thanks and warm appreciation for his work. I couldn't persuade him to let me make a copy of it.

The French ship with its "prize crew" went in convoy to England. The hardest part of all was getting to the pier at Swansea in the middle of the night, since it was pitch dark and they definitely were not expected. Fortunately, however, many of the men knew Swansea and somehow everything went well.

Sverre is now resplendent in the uniform of the Norwegian Navy and looks very military and very tanned.

25

Through Nine Concentration Camps

BY JOHN RUDOLPH RUDZIN

I was a stoker on board the S.S. *Ringulv* captained by Torvald Messel when, in convoy from Swansea to Oslo with cargo, she was turned back within a short distance of Norway's cruising waters. We were taken in to England, where along with about sixty other Norwegian ships we—now in one port now in another—lay waiting for further orders. After three weeks we were told to take our cargo of coal to Le Havre. We were reloading there for the United States when a countermand came ordering us to help evacuate some thousand civilians from Le Havre. These, stirred by gratitude, we set ashore in Brest on June 13. At Verdun Roads orders came to proceed to Casablanca, which we reached safely by ourselves on June 15.

In July the French gave up, and we were told that our ship would have to wait a little until everything had been settled. The *Ringulv* and many other Norwegian ships waited for several weeks. What did it mean? We already felt something was wrong. Why did they hold our ship? We didn't realize that France's leading persons were already Nazis and that though we were not completely under Nazis, we had partly become so. The answer was not long in coming.

One fine morning an armed French Navy man came aboard all Norwegian, Danish, and English ships and on every ship carrying an Allied flag and took out the machine part of the engines to prevent their escape. We were made prisoners of a Nazi-ruled country! We laughed a little and said: "We've been lucky all along, have never been caught by submarines, never hit by bombs, and now we are trapped by the Nazi French!" We were left on board and continued to work, but our freedom was gone! All the Norwegian and other Allied ships were held in Casablanca from the summer of 1940 until the following February. Then our ships separated. Most of them were sent to Port-Lyautey in Morocco and a few to Port Safi, ours among them, under heavy escort of warships and with only enough coal to get them to their destination.

The authorities in Port Safi offered our captain and his ship "freedom" if he would take the ship to Bordeaux. All, captain and crew, refused. The trick didn't work. So we stayed on board the *Ringulv* in Port Safi until June 17, 1941.

Before this voyage we had received a reply to our request in Rabat for permission to go to Lisbon. The answer was that under "present circumstances" we were not allowed to leave the country, but if anybody wanted to be free he could join French ships; in other words, he could go on board ships bound for Occupied France. We said, "No, thank you!"

The morning of June 17, 1941, many armed men came on board and told us to pack up and leave—ships flying the French flag were coming. We packed and left ship. While we waited, we stayed in a motorboat alongside the ship, baring our heads and singing Norwegian hymns as we watched the Free Norwegian flag go down. There were tears in the eyes of many Norwegian boys when we said a last farewell to our unlucky yet often lucky *Ringulv*. Ours was the first Norwegian ship to be taken away. She had been our home, the place where we lived, earned our bread, helped win a victory. She was being taken away by force. We were kept for some weeks in the hotels of Port Safi.

Then one morning it happened! The police ordered us to take our valises and come to the police station, where the chief of police politely informed us that because the other ships would also be taken over, there would not be enough room for us in this little town. We were therefore to be sent north to another town to live. It would be very nice there. Well, we believed, even if we didn't know just where we were going. But we didn't realize the fate that awaited us. Police in plainclothes then herded us into a bus and away we went. We arrived at Casablanca hungry, but nobody gave us anything to eat. In the evening all of us—captains, officers, full crew—were put on a train and kept under close guard by armed detectives all the way. The next morning we arrived at a small town called Tazi. There we had a big surprise —the police there only wondered about us, asking who we were and how we got there. Funny!

Some organization! Our escorts explained that we had been sent there to live, but the police knew nothing about it. While they cabled and telephoned for information about us, we were herded into the police station. We hadn't eaten for nearly twenty-four hours. We asked for food, said we were tired and hungry from travel. They answered that if we had money, they would buy something to eat. Our captain stepped forward and said: "You! You are not ashamed to speak like that to us who risked our lives to help your country! Who saved so many lives at our risk!" The captain showed the letter from the highest authorities of the Free French thanking us for saving their people. "And after this to treat us as criminals under guard and refuse to give us anything to eat— we who were your best friends a little while ago!"

After that the police conferred with each other and half an hour later they gave us food—a half sack of dry bread and a pail of water. Well, it was better than nothing, but we saw that they no longer regarded us as friends but as enemies. How faces change in this war! In the evening of the same day they herded us into some barracks in a soldiers' camp. There were no blankets, no beds—only ankle-deep dirt! Every one of us was sad and scared; we didn't know what more would be coming. Our captain was always a proud man. It affected him so much that he didn't talk to anyone—only walked around with his head bowed.

No one knew our whereabouts outside of ourselves, because no mail, telephone, or telegraph was allowed, and we were closely guarded by colored soldiers.

This was camp number 1. Next day at noon we were put on a train under strong guard and sent further north—closer to the Nazis. Late that evening we arrived at the Algerian border town of Oujda. Some high military authorities awaited us there and told our captain that we would have to rest there and that tomorrow we would be sent to Marseilles by way of Algeria. We knew what they were aiming at, and our captain refused. He got in touch with the American consul and reported to him what the authorities intended to do. The consulate protested to the authorities, and meanwhile we were left in Oujda in camp number 2.

This camp wasn't as bad as the first one. Here we were given a little food and a bed to sleep on. We were now allowed to communicate with the outside world. Another American and I, though we could not prove our citizenship because we had lost our papers, wrote to the American consul and later got an answer saying that the consulate was making all possible effort to get us released. But freedom was still far away. One thing we did gain: through the strong protests of the American office and the Norwegian representatives in Casablanca to the Vichy government we escaped being sent to Germany. After one week of waiting we were again put on a train and sent in the direction of interior Africa. On this same train were some Polish military prisoners. They had also fought as Allies for Free France and for their own country.

The next day we arrived at a small Arab village in the desert. There was an oasis there. It was unbearably hot and the air damp. We now saw the Polish prisoners of war under military discipline. We were supposed to be sent to some place farther on, but since they found out that there was neither water nor tents there (we heard they had been given away to the German military), we stepped out into the small oasis and out under the palms and waited for what would happen next. There were several hundred Jews there who had been sent back from the Sahara Desert, where they had built a railroad. They looked terrible—skinny, sick, filthy, with rags on their shoulders. Among them were many highly intelligent people, such as lawyers, jurists, and doctors. They told horrible stories of how they had been treated. Without their telling we could have seen what they had been through. In the evening we were given blankets and told to go to sleep. But where were we to go to sleep? we asked. Right on the ground under the open sky they put us, like dogs. Such hospitality from supposed friends!

The following day they told us we had to march seventy-five miles to a place in the desert where they wanted to build a camp and start making a road. Those of us who were ill, along with some old men, were taken there by truck. That was about half our number. The other half was supposed to follow a few days later, but the project never went through because such strong protests began reaching Vichy from Washington, D.C., that orders came from Moroccan headquarters at Rabat not to put us to work. Half of our crew was, however, already working hard in the desert with no shade anywhere, nothing but sand. Water was transported in large tanks and when it arrived, hot from the sun, it was rationed.

Food was scarce and on the hottest days they were given only a couple of potatoes each. They had to work from sunup to dusk. We who were left behind awaiting further orders did not work. We slept on the ground with scorpions, tarantulas, and snakes creeping all around us. For food we were given bread and warm water, but before we could get it we were forced to walk about ten miles in the desert. Meanwhile we heard that all Norwegian ships had been interned and their crews put into camps.

After about two weeks our half of the crew was sent back from the desert labor camp, and then we were sent on to the next camp, number 4. Before we left, the desert crew got their "wages" as workers in a forced-labor camp. They were one franc, twenty-five centimes a day, a total of eighteen francs, seventy-five centimes for the two weeks. That is about twenty-five cents in American money for a half month's work in the desert under unbearable climatic conditions.

We were now sent back to Casablanca by the same route we had come, and arrived there on the third day. It was early morning when we reached Casablanca with our "convoy." We looked terrible—unkempt, dirty, hungry, ill, and tired. A man from the Norwegian office came to meet us. He bought coffee and sandwiches for us and after a rest we were put on a train and once more sent to the interior of Africa. They told us this was a civilian, not a labor, camp.

The place lay about two hundred miles into the interior at a small town called Settat. There we arrived late in the evening, and walked about two miles from the town to a camp in a forest. Here we saw tents and some mud huts without windows or doors. We realized at once that this was no civilian camp but a gloomy labor camp—one of hundreds established by the Nazis in Morocco, where they forced all the ex-Foreign Legionnaires who sympathized with the Allies to work. Everything was under strict military discipline and armed French soldiers marched about brutally compelling the inmates to work. Our first work was to build a road from the highway through the forest to the camp. It was terribly hot and the work was hard. The guard didn't even give us five minutes to rest; we were now slaves in the real sense of the word under Nazi rule. The bugle blew at five o'clock in the morning. At half past five we got a cup of coffee, a small piece of bread, and a sardine, and on that breakfast we had to work until noon. Ever since we had been interned we had been hungry. We had been given only bread. Water was a delicacy! We slept right on the sand and dirt in muddy shacks without windows or doors. Rain leaked right through the mud roofs and we had no place to protect ourselves from the dampness. Days were hot and nights cold. Many, including myself, contracted malaria and one of our number died during our period in camp.

Later, more prisoners arrived and we were separated. Some were sent to work on plantations, others to work on the road, others to build houses from white rock, and some to haul rock for the building. But what hauling! We hewed out the rock with big irons and then carried it half a mile on our backs or shoulders. We had to keep going all day without stopping and the half mile was uphill all the way. Military guards were stationed at intervals and each one marked time. Whenever anyone passed whose piece of rock was too small, he was sent back. They also watched those who fell out of line, and these were punished by being deprived of several days' pay. If it happened often, the prisoner was sent into a punishment camp in the Sahara Desert. One Swede from our ship was sentenced to a punishment camp, but on the way there he jumped out of the train and was saved by the Swedish consulate in Casablanca. Later I was sent to do plantation work. We had to march three miles to work every morning, carrying our tools—picks, shovels, axes, etcetera. We also had to carry water with us. We dug holes in the ground four feet deep and four feet square for trees. Every man had to dig a certain number of holes a day or be punished. The sun was burning hot. In many places we struck rock and our hands became blistered. But we had to keep going hour by hour, day by day, month by month. Many of us became ill from the bad food and unhealthy climate. Dysentery and malaria spread.

We suffered terribly and didn't believe we would ever leave this place alive. I got malaria. The sanitation inspector, instead of sending me to a hospital, treated me on the spot, right where I lay in the dirt, and he gave me six injections in the hip. It hurt terribly and after it I had to lie down on the ground without as much as a bed. I became stiff after the injections and could scarcely walk. Even so I was forced to work. I pushed a heavy wheelbarrow full of sand and tried now and then to rest a little, but the guards kicked me brutally and warned that if I stopped once more I would be sent to a punishment camp. I gritted my teeth and carried on because the punishment camp, as we learned, was the same as a death sentence!

Meanwhile the American consulate in Casablanca and the Norwegian office did what they could to get us out of this hell and into a better camp. A great number of telegrams were exchanged between Washington and Vichy, so strong had the Nazis become in Morocco. Finally, late in the fall of 1941, we received our first good news—we would be sent to a real civilian camp near the coast to which all interned seamen had been sent.

That was the end of our worst labor camp, the fifth, but it was not the end of camps. The next day we were put into an old charcoal-burning bus about a hundred years old and shipped on to a new camp, Sidi-el-Ayachi, about sixty miles south of Casablanca. This was really our best camp. We didn't have to work and we had houses to sleep in. At first there were no beds and no blankets and we slept on the floor. Then the American consul came for inspection and after his protest the French authorities gave us beds. There were people of many nationalities interned there—women and children, most of them Jewish because the Nazis didn't like Jews. There were also many Spaniards—wives whose husbands worked in concentration camps, refugees, men who had been crippled in the Spanish civil war and were unable to work. Other Spanish refugees, thousands of them, worked out in the Sahara Desert building the trans-Saharan railroad for two cents a day!

All the interned Norwegian seamen were now together, and stayed there through the winter until the month of May. Every month we were called together and asked whether we wanted to go home and be "free." Only those seamen were asked whose country was occupied by the Germans. Everyone answered, No! Their concentration camps did not succeed in breaking our spirits. All they gained was to make us hate them more. Every one of us stood by the Allies!

At last an announcement came from the French authorities. They agreed to give all interned seamen a visa to Lisbon. Everybody was glad. Now there would be an end to camps and there would be real freedom. Arrangements were made by the Norwegian office in Casablanca and passports were issued and paid for.

A passenger boat was chartered and arrived in Casablanca; our tickets were all paid for. On the evening before our supposed departure we were called together and the commandant of the camp told us to be ready to leave early the next morning. Everyone was glad and excited—freedom at last! An hour later, that same evening, orders came to stay. Nobody was to go anywhere. The order certainly came from German headquarters in Casablanca, and once again we fell into gloom and waited and waited. The Royal Norwegian

Government lost a couple of million francs by this bluff.

One May morning all seamen were again packed into buses and sent to a new camp 150 miles into the interior of Africa. There were also a number of English prisoners. Every fifty days a German commission came for "inspection." They came from Casablanca in full Nazi dress uniform. We were invited to ask questions. No one did. Thus we lived the whole of that summer.

At the end of the summer ten interned Greek seamen managed somehow to escape. After that an especially trusted guard armed with rifle and pistol was placed over us. Barbwire was put over windows and doors. On September 6, orders came that every seaman was to be sent from Morocco to Algiers in reprisal for the escaped seamen. So once again we set out for a new camp. In Casablanca we were kept in a military camp while we waited to be transported farther. And here the American consul came and brought me the best news I had ever had. He told me that my citizenship papers had arrived from Washington and that I need not go with the other seamen to the next camp. Since it was Saturday evening, I was advised to come to the American office on Monday to get my papers. All the Norwegian seamen went to Algiers the same evening under heavy guard. The boys, I later learned, had a tough time in Algiers. They were brought to a place in the mountains far from civilization. They got very little food and no tobacco. Conditions were terrible in every way. Every day they were asked whether they wanted to go home to Nazi-occupied countries. No one gave in!

My fate was not finished when the Norwegians were sent to the next camp. I was free, as the consulate said, and on Monday I set out for the United States office to get the papers showing that I was protected. On the way to the consulate I was again arrested by the local police. They asked me my citizenship. I said I was an American and had just been released from camp. Would they please let me go to the United States office to get my papers? But they didn't listen to me. They put me in a cell to sleep on a cement floor and gave me half a pound of dry bread a day and water because I happened to be an American!

They didn't let the consulate know where I was—no one knew my whereabouts. After two days, even though I was an American citizen they sent me under guard back to the concentration camp at Sidi-el-Ajachi. From there I sent a cable to the American consulate. The American office did all in its power to obtain release for an American citizen. A month passed before the consulate succeeded in freeing me. Now I was free, yet not really free. At last, however, the French authorities agreed to give a visa to American citizens if they passed the doctor's examination and were unfit for military service. I, with other Americans, passed the examination, but of course they found me fit for military service, since the doctors were also under the Nazis. So I waited; but I didn't have to wait long before the Americans came to free us.

This story is true! It can be proved by thousands of innocent people who were interned in Morocco and now are free!

26

The Remarkable Escape of the M.S. "Lidvard"

BY BJARNE SMØRDAL

The M.S. *Lidvard* arrived at Dakar on May 30, 1940, with a cargo of rice from Saigon. Having been told that it would be unloaded in about ten days, we worked overtime in the engine room to change two bushings and to complete several other repair jobs within the allotted time. Contrary to expectations, the unloading proceeded slowly, and the battles in northern France led to the collapse of France on the very day the unloading was completed.

It was arranged that we should dock in Dakar, and the towboats came to haul us to our berth, when suddenly orders came to anchor. Later in the day, June 18, we anchored in the outer roads.

Naturally none of us even suspected that we were being interned; we thought that the dock was probably going to be used by some warship. But as the days went by, ships of many nationalities arrived. All of them eventually went to the outer harbor; and we noticed that none of them left. Altogether fifty-six ships lay anchored there at the time, including nine Norwegian, ten Greek, seven Danish, five Swedish, three English, three Polish, one Belgian, one Dutch, one Yugoslav, one Finnish, one Italian, and fourteen French.

At first they didn't keep too strict a watch on the ships, and barriers were broken at several places. Every vessel had her engines in running order; she was merely refused permission to depart. Then one day we saw one of the British vessels weigh anchor and set out to sea without a pilot on board. She did not get far, however, before she was stopped and forced to return and anchor anew. The same day the crews of all three British ships were taken ashore. The next night two Polish ships set out and on the following night the third. By then the French realized that an order not to leave was insufficient; so they came aboard and removed certain parts of the machinery from each ship. From ours they took a section of the starting pipe. Within three days, however, we had made new parts from materials we had on hand and with the parts replaced we were clear to sail at any time.

More weeks passed and then one evening the M.S. *Rolf*, a little 500-ton Dutch vessel, stole away. Her departure caused less commotion than we had expected. A few evenings later a terrible shooting set in and we noticed that a ship had got far beyond the barrier. The next morning a tug appeared hauling the 12,000-ton Belgian freighter *Carlier*. She was towed around the harbor apparently as an object lesson to the rest of us just in case we had any thoughts of leaving. She was full of holes. Several shells had conspicuously passed through the midship cabin section; hits had also been scored on the smokestack, the ventilator, and the bridge. The shipside had three large holes at the engine room, and at hold number 4 there was a hole large enough for a man to crawl through. Another shell had set fire to the cargo in hold number 7 and it burned for several days. It was said that the ship had been hit fifty times. Strangely enough, only one man was injured. The *Carlier*'s bad luck was that a big part of the barrier had got caught on her propeller, making speed impossible. Later, after the *Carlier* had been unloaded, three and a half tons of steel wire was removed from the propeller.

But this time the *navigation de police* really went into action. The engines of all the ships were to be put completely out of commission and threats were made of concentration camps and of sinking without warning should anyone attempt to sneak away. A commission of four officers arrived on board to decide what more should be removed from our engines. It was decided that the entire starting pipe should go ashore. These officers undoubtedly spoke perfect French, but unhappily for them, on that day I did not understand a word of French and so sign language was the only way out. Various pipes were pointed to with considerable gesticulation and demonstration intended to indicate that all of these should be removed and be ready for delivery that afternoon. Unfortunately, however, when they arrived to get the pipes the most important of them had not yet been taken out. I, of course, had not understood that they wanted those. I believe they gave me a calling down and I think they said they would be back later. I defended myself by saying that I was able to understand orders in six different languages but not in French and recommended that they bring an interpreter. At any rate the pipe was not taken out and the officers did not return. But they had now removed six lengths of the starting pipe and with the materials we had left, there was little prospect of our making usable replacements. Besides, we had developed respect for French shells and were constantly being assured by our Danish-Norwegian consul that it wouldn't be long before we could sail.

Thus there came a letup in our eagerness to break out of captivity and we tried to reconcile ourselves to what we regarded as our inescapable fate. During the time which followed we also had a number of experiences which provided some relief in our otherwise monotonous existence. On several occasions there were sudden outbursts of shooting overhead—British planes were out on reconnaissance.

About five o'clock one morning we heard a terrific gunfire and came up on deck to find tracer bullets flying in every direction. Shells whizzed between our mast tops. Several interned ships were hit. We didn't know what to make of it, since it was impossible to tell what was being shot at, whether planes, ships, or submarines. When day broke we saw towboats alongside the 35,000-ton French battleship *Richelieu*. After a while they towed her in to a pier in the inner harbor. The riddle was answered by a broadcast from London later in the day which said that a small English motorboat had managed to get under the stern of the *Richelieu* and drop depth bombs and that oil was floating over the water.

Since then I have had a great respect for British news bulletins, because a chance to inspect the ship more closely later proved all the statements made by London to have been accurate. Naturally we never did find out exactly how great the damage was, but it was said that one propeller was missing, that the axles of the others were bent, that the rudder had been damaged beyond repair, and that the tanks were leaking. The last could scarcely be concealed, inasmuch as the entire harbor was full of oil for several weeks afterward.

The *Richelieu* never came out of the inner harbor, and during the following six or seven months divers and work boats were constantly alongside. For extra protection she was fenced off by a double torpedo net and the buoys lay so close together that no boat could pass through except at a protected spot. After a long time they succeeded in repairing the leaks in the bottom, only to discover when the water had been bailed out that the stern lay three or four feet under the waterline.

The *Richelieu* was still at the pier during the British attacks of September 23, 24, 25. Also in the harbor at that time were two cruisers, four destroyers, three torpedo boats, an unknown number of submarines, and four or five patrol boats; all of these lay in the inner harbor.

THE BATTLE OF DAKAR

On September 23 we were awakened shortly after five in the morning by a violent shooting. Anti-aircraft cannon on the *Richelieu* and on the cruisers *Georges Lieuges* and *Montcalm* had gone into action. Planes were circling high in the sky over the city. We noticed that the shooting had no effect on the planes; they continued to circle round and round while the shells exploded far below them, or so it appeared to us.

This was just as day was breaking, so we could not see everything clearly in the beginning, but before the planes disappeared it was full daylight. By that time they had dropped thousands of leaflets reporting that General de Gaulle had come and that he would send representatives at seven o'clock to negotiate with Dakar's authorities on the matter of combining forces against Germany. The leaflets said that a small unarmed motorboat would enter the basin between piers one and two.

We saw the boat go in there at precisely seven o'clock. It flew a white flag and passed the *Richelieu* without interference. We could not see what took place in the harbor, but we were told later that the boat went directly into the basin, where the representatives of De Gaulle who were abroad met the Governor and the authorities. A discussion followed, but the authorities refused to take any action in violation of orders from Vichy. Finally the Governor pointed his revolver at the boat and declared that if the De Gaullists did not leave immediately they would be shot at. Thereupon the boat left and we saw it pass the *Richelieu* again without interference. When it was a few hundred meters beyond the breakwater, however, the *Richelieu* opened fire with a vengeance; we could clearly see the shells striking the water around the boat. But the boat continued steadily on its way and got out. Later we heard that three of its men had been killed, among them a grandson of Marshal Foch.

All this happened at about half past seven. The visibility was so poor that morning that we could not see the British warships beyond the harbor. A little after nine two torpedo boats approached the entrance, only to be driven back by heavy shooting from the *Richelieu* and from the two cruisers which had moved out to the outer roads where we lay anchored. The three destroyers and the two torpedo boats had also moved out to that position. At about ten-thirty the British warships began firing. It was plain to see that the *Richelieu*, which of course was still tied to a pier in the harbor, was the chief target of the British. The shooting must have been done from triple-cannon batteries, because three shells always arrived together. It was thrilling to see them as they fell. We do not know whether the *Richelieu* suffered any damage that day, but she probably did. I do not believe any shells fell in the city. The fortification on Cape Manuel also received several heavy salvos which sent dirt flying high in the air.

The shooting stopped at about twelve o'clock but began again at two and continued for a full hour. At five one of the destroyers, *X102*, ventured beyond the island on a scouting expedition. Before long she swung round and headed inward at full speed. But it was too late—she got a direct hit in the magazine. At that moment she was only a few ship lengths away from us. All of a sudden we saw a tremendous sea of flame around the conning tower; it looked as if the entire front of the ship was ablaze. She went aground, and later was hauled into the naval base as a wreck. Eighty-five men lost their lives. Early the next morning, September 24, the scouting planes were again overhead and at seven o'clock the cannonading began from the sea. It was steadily answered from the French side. The shooting continued with brief interruptions until three in the afternoon.

It was a disgrace to the French Navy the way its cruisers sought protection among the interned merchant vessels. The *Georges Lieuges* took position just inside the *Lidvard* and there she remained to fire her salvos right over our midship structures while the two torpedo boats circled the entire harbor laying smoke screens to hide the cruisers and destroyers. It was not a pleasant day for us. Two shells fell right near us, one to starboard and the other aport just in front of the bow of the cruiser. When we investigated the damage after the shooting was over, we discovered that only fragments of shells had struck us. I have the fragment of a shell from a twelve-inch cannon here in my cabin. It weighs four and one-half kilograms [about eleven pounds] and was sizzling hot when we found it. It lay on the forward deck near hatch number 2, where it burned a deep hole in the wood.

We fared far better, however, than some of the other ships which lay in the inner harbor near the *Richelieu*. The *Tacoma*, a Danish freighter, was set afire and was a total wreck. Four men aboard her were killed. A fire started in the Swedish *Korsholm*, but it was kept in check and the ship was towed to the outer harbor. A large French passenger liner and a smaller fruit boat were also ablaze. On the Danish ship *Australien* a piece of shell weighing twenty-three kilograms smashed one of the winches. Strangely enough, not one member of the crews of ships lying in the outer harbor was injured. It was quite revealing that all the French merchant ships weighed anchor and got out of the line of fire, while the rest of us had to stay where we were because our engines were out of commission.

We witnessed a brilliant but unsuccessful torpedo attack

which four British dive bombers directed at a French destroyer. Flying at high altitude, the planes reached their position above the outer harbor unobserved until all four, one after the other, made their dives. It was only after the first one released its torpedo that we—and the Frenchmen, too, for that matter—became aware of them. Unfortunately none of the torpedoes found its target, but it was a magnificent sight to watch the planes as they dived straight down on the destroyer and then leveled off to fly away almost touching the water and zigzagging to avoid the anti-aircraft guns which by that time had been brought into full play. All the planes got away without being damaged.

The Danish *Tacoma*, as I said, was set ablaze at her pier in the inner harbor. At the beginning we were not able to see how serious the fire was, but after it had burned a couple of hours we noticed a towboat approach the vessel and a little later pull her away from the pier. The entire midship structure was then afire, but the decks both fore and aft were still untouched. The tug fastened its hawser to the stern of the *Tacoma* in order to pull her away from the pier. What we couldn't understand was that it continued to haul the ship stern first out through the entrance to the inner harbor instead of shifting its hawser to the bow for much greater control over the wreck. Since the fire had still not reached the forepart of the ship, the change could have been made with ease. But the French tug continued towing the wreck stern first with the result that the wreck kept cutting out to the side. Since there were a great many ships anchored in the outer harbor, it was only by chance that the wreck got past without ramming them. And then instead of hauling the wreck down towards the lee and letting her drift ashore on Gory Island, the towboat attempted to haul her against the wind and in among the interned ships in order to ground her on a bank north of us. The wind was, to be sure, not very strong, but what there was was northerly and there was some sea. It didn't take long before the towrope broke—I guess four or five times. And what impressed us most during these maneuvers was the clumsy way in which the powerful tug was being used. Finally it gave up the whole attempt to ground the wreck, abandoning her a short distance north of the interned ships. It was then eight o'clock in the evening. The fire had by that time spread to both the bow and the stern. And the *Tacoma*, now all ablaze, came drifting toward the interned ships; it looked as if she was heading straight for us. How that flaming wreck drifted between all those interned ships without touching a single one is one of the most remarkable things I have ever seen. But most remarkable of all was, of course, that all members of the towboat's crew received medals for distinguished service.

THE ESCAPE
PLANNED AND EXECUTED

Along in the fall we began to doubt whether our hope of getting out of Dakar would ever be realized until the war was over unless we took matters into our own hands. The consul, who had kept telling us "it won't be long now," had been dismissed, so we were left without anyone to turn to for assistance. It was then that certain members of the crews of the Norwegian ships began laying plans for escape.

One Sunday some of our men got permission to use one of the lifeboats for a sail in the harbor. That proved to be their trial run. They were back on time in the evening and the boat was hoisted aboard. The following morning both the boat and seven men disappeared. There went all our young fellows—not one of them more than twenty years old—and the more experienced men who remained behind were pretty sure they would never get to Bathurst, a small British colony lying on the coast eighty-seven miles to the south. We did not know how they had fared until some weeks later when a broadcast from WRUL, the Boston short-wave station, informed us that they had reached their destination safely.

From then on more and more men and lifeboats disappeared, until the French authorities sent us a circular warning that if any more attempts at escape were made, all the men remaining on the Norwegian ships would be sent to concentration camps. At the same time they forbade us to put boats in the water and demanded that the tackle be removed from the davits. For any absolutely necessary transportation to any of the nine Norwegian ships we received permission to use a motorboat from the *Skotfoss,* but this, it was said, would have to be hauled up on deck every evening. Each of the Norwegian ships had a motorized lifeboat on board, but when the police demanded that all the cylinder heads from these be brought ashore, the boats were of course made useless.

Because of the severe punishment with which all of us were threatened there were no further escapes for a while, but in the spring they were on the move. Hardly a week passed that a boat or two didn't disappear. Thus in March we found ourselves without a single crew member in the engine room; even our fourth engineer had disappeared. On deck only two seamen remained. All the young men had left us, and over the radio came greetings and word from them that everything had gone according to plan. The Boston short-wave station being our chief source of information, we listened to it every day, heard all the fine speeches and reports about the great contribution Norwegian seamen were making in the Battle of the Atlantic. We heard Captain Riiser-Larsen's stirring appeal to all Norsemen outside of Norway. It made a deep impression when he asked: "What did you do for your native land? Were you far away, lapping up sunshine in South America? Or were you one of the King's men? Were you a slacker?" And we missed hardly a newscast from London.

One day early in January we heard a rumor that the French Government intended to take over the *Gabon*. There was also talk of their seizing other ships, but after all the trouble they had in getting the *Gabon* ready for use they apparently lost all interest in motor ships. They did, however, take the Danish *Australien,* sending a towboat along with her when she set out.

By this time matters had gone so far that even we who were left began to talk about escape. I did not think it would be right of me to leave the ship and explained this to Johan Karlsen, the second engineer. The two of us agreed that the *Lidvard* was far too good a ship to abandon to the French, and so we came to the conclusion that if we were to escape it would have to be with the whole *Lidvard*.

We discussed several plans for making new pipes, but our discussions always narrowed down to the fact that we lacked the necessary materials. Nor did we have enough oil to get all the way to Freetown. We had had only forty-four tons when we reached Dakar and during the past months we had been tapping this supply for both the galley and the auxiliary engine. By March we had only twenty-one tons left.

It happened that the Norwegian ship *Heimvard* was lying not far from us and from her chief engineer I learned that she had about four hundred tons of oil on board. The engineer was quite willing to let us have some of it if our two skippers gave their approval. I went to Captain Lindtner and explained that our oil would soon be gone and that within a couple of months we would have to get a new supply if we expected to have lights or to cook food on board. I suggested that he make an agreement with the captain of the *Heimvard* to bring the two ships alongside each other and have the oil pumped directly over to us.

The captain of the *Heimvard* raised a number of objections to our way of carrying out such a plan and both skippers rejected the idea of bringing the two ships together. Time went on and it looked as if we were not going to get any oil; but I had made up my mind that the *Lidvard* should be made clear for sailing and so I continued to pester Captain Lindtner with demands for more oil.

The captain called on the agent on shore to ask how such a transfer could be accomplished. He was told that if the *Heimvard* was willing to give the oil, arrangements could be made to rent one of the Shell Oil Company barges for the transportation. It then became necessary to put pressure on the skipper of the *Heimvard* again. Finally he agreed to let us have twenty tons. But this was not enough for my purpose. I insisted that we must have sixty tons, saying that there would be no sense in our having to rent a barge again within a few months. After several more weeks of negotiating it was agreed that we should have twenty-five tons of good oil and twenty-five tons of what was called slam. I figured that this, together with what we had left, would be sufficient for my plan. The barge to transport the oil was ordered to come on Monday morning; I had boarded the *Heimvard* on the Saturday preceding to settle the details with the chief engineer. On Monday morning the barge arrived and we got our oil. I have no idea how much the French authorities may have known about all this, since the whole matter was arranged by the Shell Oil Company and the agents. We had now taken our first step toward freedom.

Then we began seriously to study possibilities with respect to the starting pipes. The chief difficulty lay in the large dimensions of the pipes. The flanges are one and a half inches thick and the pipes themselves are quarter-inch material. After having searched the entire ship without finding anything usable, we at last hit upon an idea which eventually produced a happy result. In the engine room there was a piece of quarter-inch iron plate suitable for making flanges, but there wasn't enough of it since altogether we were going to need thirteen of the one-and-a-half-inch flanges. With the material we had it would be necessary to make seventy-eight of them in order to get the required thickness—six layers to a flange. Finally we discovered an old piece of plate under the prow and with it we figured we had enough. We sneaked it down to the engine room because we didn't want anyone to know what we were up to. Since all of our crew had left, there were only the four of us who had any knowledge of the plan. And it was of great importance that it should not become known on the other ships because then word of it would soon reach shore.

Next we brought down the exhaust pipe from the donkey engine and from it we cut the sections we needed. This exhaust pipe had almost the same diameter as the original starting pipes, but being made of thinner material it had a larger bore. By joining the elbow and the straight sections very carefully, we got our dummy pipe to look exactly like the original. The joining was accomplished by trimming down pieces of thinner pipe so that these would fit snugly inside the others. The ends were then brought together and the connection was welded. The resulting pipe was so firm and strong that we were sure this part of our scheme would not be discovered. Also, the flanges were made in such a way that the fraud could be detected only by very close inspection. Each of these was built up of six pieces riveted together, then scrupulously shaped, polished, and welded to the pipes. Only the weight and the paint now remained to betray the fraud. In order to make the faked pipes somewhere near the heft of the originals we filled them with grease, inserting firm plugs at each end. The original pipes had been covered with aluminum paint, but that was over two years ago; and besides, they had had the name of our ship stamped on them before they were taken ashore. We gave our dummy pipes a coat of aluminum paint and painted the name where we believed it to be on the old ones. With considerable handling and with the aid of soot from the stacks, we got the pipes to look pretty old, dulled, and scratched and marred with use.

We were now ready for the next step, which was getting the originals on board. I had long since begun to explain to the skipper that when we had lain idle for a year we would have to try to borrow the starting pipes so that we could test our engines. I began hammering away at this point again and the result was that early in June he went to the agent and presented our wish. He was told that the matter would be placed before the authorities and that we would be informed if the idea was approved. Weeks went by, but despite repeated inquiries we got no answer.

One day in the middle of July an officer came on board to question every single man about his willingness to sail under the French flag; if the man said no, he was asked where in Norway he wished to be sent in case the French authorities requisitioned the ship. All those aboard answered that they would not sail under the French flag and all refused to be sent home. I was ashore while this was happening and when I returned I found that orders had been left for me to appear at Navigation Police headquarters the next morning to answer the questions.

After having answered No to the two questions, I asked if I might speak with the chief of police. I told him that if they did not let us borrow the starting pipes now, I would not be responsible for the condition of the engines when the time came to use them. I added that the whole thing could be done in less than a day, so that if we received the pipes in the morning we would be able to return them in the afternoon. And I offered to have our men fetch the pipes and bring them back.

A few days later the agent sent word to the skipper that we could have the pipes on Tuesday, July 22, and that two officers and two soldiers would then come on board and remain on the ship as long as the pipes were there. On Tuesday morning the patrol boat came alongside and the pipes were brought on board. One of the men was a deck officer, so he seated himself in the salon. But the other was an engineer and he got into a pair of overalls and came down to the engine room along with one of the soldiers. There the two stood all the while we were mounting the pipes and testing the engines. And against my hope that they would go above when this was over, they continued to stand, conscientiously looking on as we began loosening the pipes. That my plan would succeed, now looked very doubtful, for naturally we could not exchange the original pipes with the dummies as long as they stood watching every move. But it was getting close to twelve o'clock and we arranged it so that we still had one pipe to remove when the time came to go up to dinner. But instead of going up with us as I had expected, the two guards remained standing there.

When I had finished eating, I went to the steward and asked whether our visitors were not to be given something to eat. He said that one of them had already eaten with the skipper and that he didn't know anything about the others. So I asked the steward to set a table for three in the mess hall and to go down and invite them to dinner. This was done; and no sooner had the visitors reached the deck than we hurried below, removed the last pipe, hastily brought out the dummies and carried them up on deck, and just as hastily hid the originals. When the guards had finished their dinner, I went in and told them that all the pipes had been brought up on deck.

We had completed the job ahead of time. Since the patrol boat was not due yet, it was decided that we should bring the pipes ashore in a motorboat which we had standing on deck. They were placed in the bow. For a moment the suspense was awful when the visiting engineer walked over and looked at them. But apparently all he did was to count them, and then he seated himself in the stern.

It had been my intention to send as many of our men as possible with the boat in order to conceal the pipes and thus prevent the officers from studying them too closely during the trip to shore. I also wanted our men to carry the pipes so that the Frenchmen would not have a chance to discover that the pipes were a few kilograms lighter in weight than those they had brought out. But the plan was blocked when Captain Lindtner appeared and said there were plenty of men on shore to carry the pipes, and the two officers agreed with him wholeheartedly. Other than those of us in the engine room there wasn't a soul, not even the skipper, who knew at that time what had taken place. Thus it was that Karlsen was the only man from our ship to make the trip to shore, but upon his return he reported that everything had gone beautifully. Then after two days had passed without hearing anything from shore, we regarded it as a sure sign that all was well.

On Thursday evening some of the skippers from other interned Norwegian ships were visiting Captain Lindtner and I was present. As usual there was a good deal of talk about the latest escapes in lifeboats and while we were on that subject I spoke up.

I said, "Well, I too am now pretty well fed up with lying here in Dakar and want to get out, but when I leave I'd prefer it to be with the whole *Lidvard.*" This was taken as a joke and I was asked whether I would start the engines with a crank.

The following morning, Friday, I went to Captain Lindtner and told him what we had done and declared that the engines could be ready for leaving at an hour's notice. I also told him that no one but the four of us in the engine room knew about it, but that I was certain he would have all the others with him if he wanted to set out. We talked for a quarter of an hour, and the last thing he said was that the whole thing was hopeless. He then went ashore. About five o'clock he was back and had brought with him Captain Breivik of the *Hadrian,* Captain Nielsen of the *Skotfoss,* and Captain Ryers of the *Carlier.* I was told that it had been decided we would leave Saturday evening and that Breivik and Nielsen would come with us. Both of their ships had been taken over by the Frenchmen and they, together with the remainder of the crews, had been living aboard the *Duala.*

This hasty move was not according to my plan, since I still had various matters to attend to on shore. For one thing the crankshaft for the auxiliary engine was in a repair shop, and two of our acetylene-gas cylinders were on shore being refilled. But I realized that it was now or never—that if we didn't take this chance, there'd be none later. I therefore went ashore early Saturday morning. First I rode to the repair shop, which was outside the city, and explained that I would have to take the crankshaft back to the ship temporarily. And I got it, though I am sure it must have seemed strange to them that I absolutely had to have the crankshaft on a Saturday noon. Then I went to get the compressed-air cylinders, only to find that by mistake they had been filled with carbonic acid [carbon dioxide]. The men regretted the mistake and would be willing to empty the cylinders and fill them with acetylene gas the following week. That infuriated me and I insisted that I would not let them have anything more to do with the cylinders and would take them back to the ship with me right away.

"But can you use the carbonic acid?" they asked me.

"No, I can't!" I stormed. "But to hell with that. The cylinders are worth a lot more to me than the stuff in them." The light probably dawned on them the next morning.

On the trip back I learned that twenty-one men from the M.S. *Salta* were planning to escape that night in a lifeboat. I pictured these men as constituting our new crew, if everything went according to plan. On board our own ship I learned further that three of our men were planning to leave in the same lifeboat. I went to the captain and told him about it. Along in the afternoon the three were told about our plan, and all agreed to go with us. It was also planned that we would invite Njøten, chief engineer of the *Hadrian*, and Kristen of the *Skotfoss*, together with a steward and two seamen from these ships, to join us, though we did not mention the matter to them until later.

There were two torpedo nets around the entrance to the harbor. The inner one extended in a curve from Gory Island to some shallows beyond land in the direction of Rufisque. The outer one was much longer, since it began on the coast south of the city and stretched in a great arch nearly all the way to land at Rufisque. The location of these nets was well known to us from our fishing trips, but just to be safe we had them checked again on Saturday morning by all the skippers, and it was decided that we should go around them. The regular ship entrance in the nets was closed every evening at seven o'clock. There were almost always one or two patrol boats lying at anchor during the night, either just beyond or between the nets. And during recent weeks we had observed that a submarine was also stationed there. The destroyers, however, had various anchoring places, so we never knew exactly where they would be; they did, we noticed, frequently move into the harbor on Saturdays, supposedly to give the men shore leave. On this particular Saturday morning they were anchored inside the nets a short distance from our bow, and we were kept in great suspense as to whether they would remain there during the night. It was as if luck was with us. About four o'clock both destroyers weighed anchor and moved in to the mooring near the piers in the innermost part of the harbor. And the strange thing was that we saw none of the patrol boats set out that day. We were anxious about this and kept constant watch, but at seven we saw the towboat go out to close the nets.

And then came the excitement with the lifeboats. During March we had stowed our two remaining lifeboats in the hold. Members of the crew had already taken two of our boats to Bathurst. When it was decided that we should set out, the two lifeboats were brought up on deck and made ready in case something should happen to us during the flight. We still do not know whether the Frenchmen had discovered this and had become apprehensive. Just as I was about to go to the mess hall I noticed Karlsen standing way out at the end of the deck astern, looking intently toward land.

I went over to him, and he asked: "Isn't that the police boat way in there?"

It was clear that the boat was heading directly toward us. So they had discovered our trick with the pipes, had they? The installation of the original pipes had been completed only an hour before—now there was real danger afoot. Without wasting a moment we ran down and began loosening the pipes, although we quickly realized that it would be hopeless to try to get them all down during the short time allowed, as the boat kept coming nearer. When I had got two pipes down, I ordered the other men to continue with the work until I sent word. Then I returned to the deck to keep an eye on the boat. As soon as it was under our stern I hurried below. Only three of the pipes had been removed and these we quickly hid. Then we shut off the auxiliary engine and closed the skylights so that the engine room was completely dark. I changed the cells in my pocket flashlight to two that were nearly dead and made ready to use this particular flashlight when it came to showing them that the pipes were still missing.

I didn't have much hope of succeeding in this, but I had no alternative. We went up to the mess hall to eat but didn't have much appetite. The police were now on board and every moment I expected to hear them coming toward us. Minutes seemed hours, but no one came. We didn't dare go out on deck because we were so sopping wet with perspiration that that alone would have betrayed that something mysterious was going on.

Finally the third mate came in and told us that the officials were removing all the loose equipment in the lifeboats. This was reassuring, though I could not get myself to believe that they would not go down to the engine room. A little while later, however, word came that the officials were saying good-bye and when we thereupon ventured out on deck they were already in the boat. They had stripped the lifeboats of oars, masts, sails, rudders, and compasses. We saw them set their course toward the *Heimvard,* supposedly for the purpose of making the same kind of raid there.

It had been agreed that the men who were to accompany us and who were now on board the *Duala* should come over and join us after nightfall. They had been ready to start, when they saw the police boat come alongside us. Upon seeing what happened to all our lifeboat equipment, they were convinced that the whole plan had been discovered. Captain Breivik and Nielsen, the mate, then set out from the *Duala* in a motorboat in an attempt to come over and find out how matters stood. They had hoped to sneak by to port of the *Heimvard* just as the police boat tied up on starboard. But they were seen and commanded to stop. Captain Breivik was ordered aboard the police boat, while Nielsen was sent directly to shore to report to harbor police headquarters and to remain there for the night.

Having removed the equipment from the lifeboats in all four of the Norwegian ships, the police headed shoreward.

The men on the *Duala* had by now given up all hope of realizing the carefully planned escape. When one of our lifeboats came alongside about nine o'clock, they were all in bed. The fact was that we had four oars on the rafts on the afterdeck, and these the Frenchmen had overlooked. Those four oars were enough for us to man a lifeboat, so in spite of everything we were able to get our men with us.

Toward midnight we again made the engines ready for departure. At six minutes past twelve we weighed anchor, and orders came over the telephone for full speed ahead. We did not use the telegraph because the sound of the bells would carry much too far. All deck lights were put out, and soon we were heading for sea along the inner net.

Undoubtedly there were many on the other ships who were awakened by the noise of our engines and propeller. One of the Greek ships turned her flashlights on us. Fortunately none of the goings on were observed by the Frenchmen and we went ahead full speed. When about twenty minutes had gone by and those of us in the engine room believed we had passed the nets, orders came to slacken speed and a little later to stop the engines. Those were exciting moments for us who naturally had no opportunity to keep posted on what was taking place above; every second we expected to hear a shell crashing into the side of the ship. But nothing happened. The third engineer was sent up to get information and a little later he returned to tell us that we had rounded the first net and were at that moment in the process of slipping across the second. It was also a relief to hear that no searchlights had come into action. About a minute later we received orders for full speed ahead, and then we knew to our very great joy that the nets had been left behind.

Yes, it was full speed, you can take my word for it. The engines were racing at an R.P.M. which I would never have risked under ordinary conditions. Normally, with a clean bottom the *Lidvard* in ballast makes about fourteen and one-half knots. I realized that we could not approach anything like that speed with a six-inch coating of barnacles on the ship's bottom and propeller, but I did think that with such strenuous driving we ought to make at least ten. I was therefore completely disappointed when I came on deck a little later and looked over the side of the ship. Actually we appeared almost to be standing still and to be pulling the whole ocean along with us. The night was very dark and there was considerable phosphorescence in the water. The combination served to make it look as if we were getting nowhere at all. I went up on the bridge and learned that we were making an estimated speed of about seven knots. Well, there was nothing to do about it. After four hours' running straight out to sea, we could still see the shore lights.

This was Sunday morning. We continued straight ahead until noon, when we turned southward. It looked as if our speed was improving a little as the day wore on. Without forcing the engines so desperately, we were getting up to eight knots. Apparently the outer layers of barnacles on the ship's bottom and especially those on the propeller had been worn away. We posted two watches, since the two chief engineers, Njöstein [sic] and Kristian [sic], had declared themselves willing to take a hand. The weather was clear and calm and Sunday passed quite peacefully. About five o'clock in the afternoon Captain Lindtner invited everyone in for a drink. It was with genuine champagne that we toasted each other and drank to a happy outcome for our adventure. All the men were able to join in this little ceremony, since we relieved one another for the occasion.

But it turned out that we had congratulated ourselves too soon. Only a short while afterwards we noticed a vessel on the horizon to starboard coming toward us. We veered off immediately and a little later the vessel signaled us to stop. We signaled back asking who she was but got no answer. In a few minutes she began firing at us, and we could now see that it was a ship of the trawler type, though we could not make out her nationality. The shooting convinced us, however, that it must be a Frenchman in search of us and that it was up to us to get away. Our engine, which had been giving good service earlier in the day, was now called upon to deliver even more. Signals began sounding from the bridge. The trawler was gaining on us. We stepped up the pressure. More signals. The trawler was holding us. We opened up still more. The trawler was falling behind. We were saved! I am inclined to believe that she became frightened when we established radio contact with Bathurst and Freetown. She chased us for about forty-five minutes, and when I came up on deck I heard that she had sent five shots after us but that only one of them had struck anywhere near us.

We continued southward, and the next morning, Monday, we again saw a ship on the horizon, this time dead ahead of us. She approached with terrific speed and we were well aware that, regardless of her intentions, we could not get away from her. A few minutes later signals appeared and we rejoiced when we were able to identify the British naval ensign. The ship came alongside and asked us who we were and where we were from. Evidently it was difficult for the officers to understand that we had come from Dakar; for they asked us several times to repeat it. When they finally did understand it, they shouted: "We will escort you to Freetown."

With that the most important phases of our experience were over. We reached Freetown the following evening. Later we received information that a submarine and two planes had been sent in search of us, but believing that we were headed for Bathurst, which is much closer to Dakar, they had patrolled nearer the coast. In Freetown we met the *Para,* and members of her crew told us that a large French submarine had come alongside their ship when she was only a few miles from Bathurst. The sub had approached at great speed, but the *Para* had kept her cannon aimed at her. The water was so shallow there that the submarine could not submerge and after a short time she headed out to sea again.

And then there were the twenty-one men from the *Salta* who had also planned to leave Dakar the evening we left. They had everything in readiness in their lifeboat when they saw the police boat approach the *Lidvard* about six o'clock in the evening. They noticed that the Frenchmen took all our lifeboat equipment. When the same thing happened to theirs, they gave up all thought of escaping. But their restlessness was so great that along in the evening they began working out a new plan. They found an iron pipe which could be used as a mast, a tarpaulin which could be used as a sail, and some old oars which the Frenchmen had overlooked. They were so preoccupied with all this that they did not even notice that the *Lidvard* had left. Nor had they any suspicion that such a thing was even going to take place. But having somehow or other got the impression that we had set out in our lifeboats anyway, they decided to make the attempt themselves. They sailed and rowed for two days before reaching Bathurst. A British warship brought them to Freetown, and here they shipped with us. They were just the men we needed.

Antarctica

~~~~~~

27

Norwegian Wartime Whaling

BY ARNE VIKESTAD

On board the "Thorshammer," March 21, 1941

Whales, whales, and more whales. A war raged, danger threatened—all seemed to have become remote. Out on the whaling grounds it was work, eat, sleep, work, eat, sleep. The vital consideration was the production of the largest possible volume of oil. It meant hanging on now that it was right in the middle of the season, the weather good, the whale plentiful. Later on bad weather would come and then it would be well to have an extra supply to go on. The catcher boats sped out and back with whale, announced whale by radio, a herd of them, made inquiry as to whether much whale was being seen, and so on. And the factory ship kept up a constant signaling of her bearings, calling for more and more whale. In short, everything was proceeding as usual with the whale catch.

By January 14 the floating factory *Thorshammer* had about 57,000 tanks of whale oil. The tanker *Solglimt* had just brought her fuel oil and provisions, had got 22,000 tanks of whale oil in exchange and had moved on to the factory ship *Ole Wegger,* which lay 180 miles east. Our ship was through with the transport for this time and we were well satisfied.

Our catch had been good, we had finished a little ahead of the two other Norwegian expeditions, the *Ole Wegger* and the *Pelagos,* which lay another 100 miles still farther east. Our *Thorshammer* had whale alongside, the factory was going full blast, all of our catcher boats had reported no fewer than three whales each. Prosperity!

It was almost 7:30 in the evening. The day shift was about to leave and the night shift would soon take over. The men were happy, the day had been strenuous. No stoppage. Day and night . . . one continuous round. Then two boats approached, the one a little ahead of the other. Their course was set directly on the *Thorshammer,* and the dreadful speed of the leader was noted. "It doesn't have whale," someone remarked. Another was sure "there must have been an accident on board and it wants a doctor." Coming full speed, the leader headed up to the bridge of our ship. A voice boomed through a megaphone: "Turn off your radio—get going—the Germans have seized *Wegger* and *Solglimt.* You will be told in writing." It is Kjellström on *Globe VIII,* one of the *Wegger* catcher boats. He swings round the bow, heads toward midship and delivers a letter. The other boat has now arrived. It is *Thorarin,* another of the *Wegger* catchers.

If lightning had struck, we couldn't have been more dumbfounded. A sickening feeling of disaster stunned all of us— almost like that of April 9. After a moment or two when we couldn't think, our minds came to again. We must get away— that was imperative. The engineer hurried through the factory. "Shut off the steam." Everything was stopped where before motors, crushers, boilers, presses, separators, had been going full force. The steam was now to be saved for the engine.

A second command followed. It was about the whale we had on both sides of the ship. "Haul up as much as possible on the ramp." It took too much time. "Leave all of it." The sides were cleared of whale instantly. The ship vibrated—we were in motion, bent on making all the speed we could muster. Which course to take? Southward into the ice. A small catcher boat was lying alongside us bunkering. It had got some fuel but was not through and had to leave with what it had. Another of our catcher boats had arrived with whale. This made two accounted for, but we had five more. How to warn them? We had a so-called war code under which we had agreed to send out certain numbers by radio when there was danger. This was done. Then there was the question of the lifeboats now lashed to the davits in a line along the top of the bulwarks, some of them loaded with a variety of things. We might need them. They were cleared, speedily swung free and completely checked for inventory. That took care of the lifeboats. Only one thing remained: to get away. We started, fleeing full speed south and a little to the west.

What about what we had on board uncared for? A whole whale, blubber, meat, bone? Let it lie. Nothing was touched; no kettle was emptied; the radio was shut off; all listening use of private or mess-hall radios was prohibited. Nothing must give our pursuer a clue to the direction we were taking. Only the receiver in the radio room was on. The operator heard that some of our catchers were confused and were asking for an explanation. "Shut up!" said one of the gunners in the telephone. He had been in when Kjellström arrived. Nothing beyond this curt reply.

Presently Kjellström arrived on the bridge to ask if we couldn't alert the third factory ship, *Pelagos,* now calling the *Solglimt* to say she was on the way to meet her. *Pelagos* was low on fuel and *Solglimt* was bringing it. This of course meant, he said, that *Pelagos* was heading right into the trap; for the German raider was now with the *Ole Wegger* and *Solglimt.* But our position on the *Thorshammer* being the farthest west meant that any message sent by us would only tell the German that we had been informed and knew the worst. She could take our bearings again and could certainly do twice our speed. The commander shook his head. "No, we can't do it," he called back to Kjellström. A new heaviness oppressed us—a pity we couldn't warn the *Pelagos*, which was still free. But we consoled ourselves with the possibility that one of the *Wegger* catchers had escaped and could manage an alert.

Meanwhile more and more of our *Thorshammer* catchers came in, until finally only two were missing, and they showed up later.

A thick, drifting snow was now falling. We were traveling full speed, flanked by catcher boats, and nearing the ice field. The situation confronting us was by no means a new one. The Germans, we reckoned, would now find it difficult to follow us. With the ice and a heavy snowfall this was our chance. We traveled in this manner until two o'clock in the morning. Then we encountered heavy floating ice, making it impossible to get farther south. After a brief conference we set our course for South Georgia Island and were there in five days. Three days earlier, however, we had sent one of our catchers in advance with a written notice from our commander to the magistrate of South Georgia advising him of what had happened.

The catcher boat had reached the island early Sunday morning. The station was asleep. The catcher boat tooted. A sleepy watchman appeared and took charge of the mooring. What kind of vessel was this flying the flag of Norway aft and all signal flags flying? A brief explanation and the station came to life. The magistrate was aroused, read the notice, had a brief conference with the messenger. The telegraph dispatched the information to Falkland and from there it went to other places.

Now for the first time the world was to learn what had happened in the South Atlantic in January. After we had pulled ourselves together a little, we began to wonder how the catcher boats *Globe VIII* and *Thorarin* had come out of it. We got the story. In the gray of dawn *Globe VIII* was on its way to the *Ole Wegger* with two whales when it heard the voice of its director calling to each of the catchers individually to come in and deliver its catch and to wait for further orders. This had struck Kjellström as being somewhat remarkable. When, therefore, he came near enough to see the *Wegger* through the telescope and to investigate, he discovered a third ship of about 12,000 tons armored with cannon lying alongside the *Wegger* and *Solglimt*. On second thought he recalled that the familiar voice of director Evensen had sounded strange and also that it had summoned a catcher which late that evening had already reported that it had no whale. Good advice was at a premium. That the raider could see both the catcher boat which was without any whale and the *Thorarin* coming in to the factory was a certainty. Kjellström had his wits about him. He disposed of his whales, reported to the *Wegger* that he was in pursuit of blue whales, veered off a distance, got under the lee of an iceberg, reported that he had caught fish, then a little later that his fishline had got tangled in the propeller, that he needed help, and called the *Thorarin* to come to his assistance. The *Thorarin,* unaware of the ruse, came. Kjellström told *Thorarin* what he had seen— a 12,000-ton passenger or combination passenger and cargo ship. Evidently, therefore, a German raider. His uneasiness had increased upon hearing a Norwegian voice with a marked German accent speaking in the *Wegger*'s telephone. It was then they agreed to head for the *Thorshammer* and alert her to the danger. Having heard the *Thorshammer*'s bearing, they sped with all their might to reach her. At about 7:30 P.M., January 14, they made it. Nice work by Kjellström. Some of the men proposed enthroning him "shoulder high."

The following Sunday, the nineteenth, we were close to

South Georgia; and during the night we reworked and adapted our original plan, which had in fact been lying just as we had left it that Tuesday evening. During the night we rode at anchor out in the harbor and Monday forenoon we went to Grytviken and anchored there. Two hours later one of our missing catchers arrived and in a couple of days the remaining one came. They had been so short of fuel that they had been compelled to go slow. Now the whole of the *Thorshammer* expedition was assembled and along with it three of the *Ole Wegger* catchers.

Yes, and still another of the *Wegger* boats, the *Pol 7,* came in to Grytviken. We learned its story. Sometime between midnight and one o'clock that Tuesday morning it had been lying alongside the *Wegger* taking on fuel. *Solglimt* too lay alongside. On the *Pol 7* the night shift was at dinner. When a dark shadow came gliding by in front of the *Wegger*'s bow, the *Pol 7* left the side. Suddenly a searchlight flashed, probably to see whether *Wegger* and *Solglimt* had cannon. Then full lights came on. Men at cannons and machine guns were pointing at the people on the *Wegger* and *Solglimt,* whose only defense was their flensing knives—of little consequence against machine guns and cannon. The Germans boarded the *Wegger* and seized both her and *Solglimt.*

The men on *Pol 7* shuddered—this was awful! What action to take? Various ones were discussed. Should they try ramming the raider broadside at full speed in an effort to puncture her? The proposal was summarily dismissed. It wouldn't work. But they did have to try to get away—that was imperative. They veered cautiously, almost imperceptibly. The Germans must not see that they were moving. In this way they managed to slip out. A snow squall came. Full speed ahead instantly—the chance had to be taken. Once the raider's searchlight passed the stern. Before the squall had blown itself out, they had got so far away in the darkness that they could not be seen and all went well. They knew nothing about the fate of the others. They thought one or more of the boats might have taken a chance during the snow squall, but how it turned out no one knew.

Radio News, London, December 22, 1941—

According to the *Day's News*, Stockholm, the Prize Court in Hamburg has awarded the German Reich the Norwegian whaling factory *Ole Wegger*, together with three catcher boats *Pol 8*, *Pol 10*, and *Torlyn*, captured in Antarctica.

Letter from the British Admiralty to Nortraship, London—

I have been instructed by the Commissioners of the British Admiralty to inform you that it has been our pleasure to read a report of the remarkable performance of Captain Kjellström, who was the captain and gunner on the catcher-boat *Globe VIII* of the *Ole Wegger* floating factory, in himself having eluded capture as a prisoner when his factory-ship was sunk by a raider January 14 and in alerting the factory-ship *Thorshammer* and its catcher-boats.

Captain Kjellström's presence of mind and prompt action saved three ships from destruction, and I ask you to convey to him an expression of the Admiralty's recognition of his outstanding achievement.

(From *Reports From the Director of Shipping*, August 5, 1941.)